THE CONTEMPORARY DISCUSSION SERIES

THE DEFENSE
OF GOD

THE
DEFENSE
OF
GOD

EDITED BY
JOHN K. ROTH
AND
FREDERICK SONTAG

A NEW ERA BOOK

PARAGON HOUSE
New York

Published in the United States by
Paragon House Publishers
2 Hammarskjold Plaza
New York, NY 10017

A New Ecumenical Research Association Book

Library of Congress Cataloging in Publication Data
Main entry under title:

The Defense of God.

(God, The Contemporary Discussion Series)
"A New ERA book,"
Includes index.
1. God—Congresses.   I. Roth, John K.
II. Sontag, Frederick.   III. Series.
BT102.A1D37   1985   291.2'11   84-25592
ISBN 0-913757-26-8 (hardbound)
ISBN 0-913757-27-6 (softbound)

Contents

Introduction

JOHN K. ROTH
AND
FREDERICK SONTAG

George Orwell projected what might happen in *1984*. In fact, he summed it up in one grim image. Winston Smith, the novel's protagonist, has no belief in God, but he does profess faith in "the spirit of Man." Soon, however, Winston will be broken. O'Brien, his interrogator, aims to insure that Winston learns to love Big Brother. Winston once thought O'Brien was his friend, but that hope shatters when the "friend" turns out to be one of the most cunning members of the Thought Police. A specialist in the subtleties of betrayal and human domination, O'Brien has less use for God than Winston does. As for Winston's faith that "the spirit of Man" will prevail, O'Brien gives a blunt rebuttal: "If you want a picture of the future, imagine a boot stamping on a human face— forever."[1]

The year 1984 began rather differently for the contributors to this book than *1984* ended. We met in Puerto Rico and occupied a conference room, not a torture chamber. There was no "trampling on an enemy who is helpless."[2] Dialogue, not domination, was our business. One hundred forty-five scholars from thirty countries had traveled to Dorado Beach for the third annual conference on "God: The Contemporary Discussion." Among the seven groups at the conference sponsored by the New Ecumenical Research Association (New ERA), one focused on "The Defense of God." That seminar, organized and moderated by Steven T. Katz and Frederick Sontag, generated the essays published here.

Our discussions were as free as the locale was beautiful. No one mentioned O'Brien and his "boot stamping on a human face." But we were preoccupied with the forces that lay waste to the human spirit, mocking everything sacred in the process. The insidious destructiveness of those powers revealed itself more intensely through the contrast between the suffering that scars the world and the civility we experienced.

The seminar's theme had been set by Sontag's plenary address at the second "God Conference." He suggested then that the human spirit is in peril because all religious life exists under the threat of destruction. He urged a defense of the divine traditions in every land. As Sontag's lead essay indicates, this situation demands "the defense of God." Yet that task is easier said than done. God is not readily defended in a world that contains so many boots stamping on so many human faces. God, moreover, says little in his own defense. Provoked by that puzzling fact, Sontag argues that the defense of God depends on what we say and do, an awesome responsibility. He concludes that God's present inaction can be defended only if God acts differently in the future than he has in the past or present. Our fate hinges on the promise that God's future holds.

Sontag's theses set the stage for the responses contained in the following pages. Although each shares Sontag's concern to revitalize religion as a means to defend the human spirit, not all accept the particulars of his account. Adrio König, for example, does not think that men and women are especially called to defend God. Nor does he think Sontag correctly appraises the silence of God. Defending his view of Christian revelation, König portrays a biblical God who not only makes himself manifest, but does so in a way that makes God's defense of the defenseless primary.

König's essay is based on a biblical theology that forces metaphysical reflection into the background. Bowman L. Clarke reverses that relationship in his "Whiteheadian Theodicy." Agreeing with Sontag that an adequate theological perspective requires philosophical grounding, Clarke also suggests that a defensible God can be found. To locate such a God, however, one must discriminate among the kinds of evil and state how God might relate to them. Clarke identifies three sorts of evil: those due to human finitude, those that result from free moral decisions, and those resulting from environmental structures. Drawing on Whitehead's philosophy, he portrays a God who always does the best God can. He lures "creatures to actualize the better alternatives." God seeks "everlastingly . . . to overcome evil in the world."

Lloyd Eby concurs. God is good, and God can be defended.

Eby's approach, however, cuts between those of König and Clarke. In drawing on the revelation found in Unification thought, he is committed to articulate a metaphysical view. Acknowledging that Unification theology has much in common with Whitehead's process philosophy, Eby feels that the former is superior, even though "Unification texts or official writings do not contain an explicit theodicy." He tries to fill that gap by developing a Unification defense of God in the face of evil. God's power is interpreted in such a way that "evil is not something that God creates or is responsible for." This outcome links the essays of Eby and Clarke but leaves both of them at odds with Sontag's.

Neither metaphysics nor revelation occupies center stage in Frank R. Harrison's essay, "On Hearing God." Struck by the cacophony of religious claims, he explores "the thesis that God is continually speaking to us but it is we who are not listening to him." The problem, Harrison believes, is that we tend to employ epistemological assumptions that make it difficult, even impossible, to catch God's word. Those assumptions involve a world view that places a premium on objectivity and instrumental value. Finding those emphases inadequate, Harrison's contribution is an alternative approach that may help us understand "science and ordinary matters-of-fact in our daily lives" and God as well.

The defense of God, Jörg Salaquarda reminds us, requires a defense of religion. The power of religion in human life is still impressive. Partly because of that fact, religion remains a target. This is understandable, says Salaquarda, for religion often supports questionable causes, and its authority in speaking for God is often in doubt. Nonetheless, Salaquarda's essay argues that some religions are better than others. The right kind of religion, in fact, is indispensable to establish "a successful and liberating coordination of human powers." He develops this view by examining various forms of what he calls "the argument of repression." In brief, this argument holds that religion is one of the boots that stamps on human faces. Salaquarda believes that charge is justified at times, but not always. Our need is to develop self-critical forms of religion that help the human spirit.

Martin Prozesky advances Salaquarda's goals. Like Harrison, he is troubled by the dissonance that results from a host of competing religious claims, especially when each one tends to assert that its view alone contains the truth. But if Harrison finds an epistemological quest for objectivity too confining, Prozesky thinks that religious harmony and insight are sapped by a glut of subjectivism. He, too, offers an alternative approach—one that provides a set of criteria to evaluate religious claims. Prozesky hopes these criteria are reasonable enough to win the agreement of all who think critically. He wonders whether any religious tradition can be found that meets the criteria he sets forth. But his "Judging Religion" remains hopeful, because he believes that its criteria can help "to develop a planetary religious reality—to find the global amidst the deceptively regional, the supremely worthy amidst the relatively good, the jewel within the lotus."

Klaus A. Rohmann's perspective is different, although not completely so. He remains skeptical about the possibility of obtaining a single set of criteria we can all agree to use in judging religion. The difficulty, Rohmann suggests, is that human understanding has been relativized. As self-reflective beings, we have learned that experience yields perspectives that differ. This aspect of us makes a defense of either God or religion problematic, because the base on which such a defense can be mounted remains uncertain. Rohmann's conclusion, however, is not despairing. The need for religious defense is more, not less, important owing to the influence of what Rohmann calls "perspective thinking." Thus, he urges a return to reflection on the world-as-creation. That ancient perspective, with its implications concerning God and the need for a spiritual response from God's creatures, could stall O'Brien's future.

Distressed by religion's contributing "more to human disarray than to human solidarity," Eugene T. Long adds his perspective to themes stressed by Prozesky and Rohmann. Admitting that historical and cultural differences limit "efforts to give a final account of the being of human existence," Long nevertheless argues that humanity transcends these particularities. What he calls "the ontological map" of human existence can at least be sketched. By seeing how the world's religious traditions fit upon it, Long adds, we can better understand how their categories function, and appraise whether some of those categories are more sensible than others. One way to start this inquiry involves paying attention to *commitment*. It appears to be an essential ingredient in every view of a fully human existence. When religious traditions interpret commitment, says Long, they tend to emphasize the importance of "trust in reality." By building on the ways in which diverse religious paths share "confidence that somehow things are all right," he believes we may mount a defense of God that strengthens social solidarity.

Subtitling his essay "A Reprise," John K. Roth returns to a theme already stated. He does so by echoing Sontag's challenge: Many defenses take God off the hook too easily. But the meaning of "a reprise" also has roots in "taking back." Roth's essay focuses on the Holocaust, the Nazi attempt to exterminate the Jews of Europe, and on religious responses to that event. It urges a "taking back" in the sense that we must be careful not to defend God at humanity's expense. Even the call to defend the divine traditions in every land must guard against that danger. In exploring how to maintain such vigilance, we should learn "not to say too much—or too little—in the defense of God."

If this book succeeds in doing what its title suggests, contributing to the defense of God, that will happen because each reader wrestles with the fact that there are conflicting views of God in these essays. The authors do not see eye-to-eye on where the greatest religious insights are to be found. But even in the disagreement there is a shared concern that boots must not stamp on human faces and there is a conviction that the health of religion, and therefore the defense of God, can make crucial contributions toward that end. The essays were written with such goals in mind; they are published with the hope that progress toward them will occur. Their test is in the reading, to which you are invited.

NOTES

1. George Orwell, *1984* (New York: New American Library, 1983), 220. The novel was originally published in 1949.
2. Ibid.

1

The Defense of God

FREDERICK SONTAG

In modern times theologians have differed as to whether or not God is all-powerful (omnipotent). Still, few have ever doubted that if a Divinity can be said to exist, it is at very least the most powerful being in the universe. To be responsible for the creation of galaxies and planets such as we inhabit, let alone control every human activity, requires immense power. Moreover, most people think that God, or the supreme Divinity, works to achieve good in the world. Destructive forces are all around us. But even if they are not now under direct divine care, we picture God as possessing the power and the ability to control them where and when he chooses.

All this involves the age-old problem of theodicy. If God is that Being than which nothing more powerful can be conceived (to paraphrase Anselm), given his good intentions for his creatures, why does he not intervene to protect them and promote their good against every threat? That is an important question, and the answer we give hinges both on our notion of God's intentions and on his use of power. However, although it has not often been mentioned, what I want to stress is that God's failure to defend himself against attack is even more puzzling. Countless theodicies have been written to explain why God seldom protects helpless human beings from catastrophe, but little has been done to explore the divine reason for God's failure to provide for his own defense against the attacks that have been made upon him.

The Indecisive Situation

If the actions of human beings often offend him or thwart his plans, the standard response has been to say that God prizes human freedom and will not interfere with it, even though the price for such abstinence is high. This explanation is full of difficulties, at least two of which are: (1) the meaning of freedom, which is seldom agreed upon; and (2) the question of whether sufficient human freedom might be allowed and yet we could still exercise our volition with considerably less destructive effect. But again I want to suggest that God's failure to speak out in his own defense is even more difficult to explain. In dealing with this, Judaism has its own special problem centering on Israel's covenanted relationship to God, but let us use Christianity, with which I am more familiar, as an example.

God appears very little in the New Testament, except in the voice heard with the dove's descent at the time of Jesus' baptism. Of course, one might argue that God was evident in his action to raise Jesus from the dead, following which the Holy Spirit did descend upon the early disciples with the result of reshaping their dispirited zeal into an expanding church. A voice to Peter did command him to eat "unclean" food, and this released Christianity to become an international religion no longer confined within the Mosaic law. Even so, neither God's voice nor his actions are seen or heard in the New Testament in his own defense. Why? If Christians believe that Jesus came among us as God's incarnated presence, at least in that life we might expect to find God's self-defense prominent. But a reading of the Gospels leaves almost the opposite impression. Jesus seems defenseless and even unwilling to protect his divine mission from attack. He evidences little concern to defend himself.

Why should this be so? If God decided to enter the world to accomplish his will among men, as Christians assert, then why did he not do so with a show of force appropriate to the immensity, if not the omnipotence, of his power? If we read the temptation stories, which concern the testing of Jesus' intentions as he begins his ministry, the moral we can draw is that Jesus felt impelled to take a harder path than the easy way he was tempted to use. He rules out the unleashing of a display of divine power to overwhelm the opposition as too simple. But why not use every weapon you possess to promote a divine plan? If our motives and intentions are good, why should we use anything less than the full power at our command? It seems foolish to lose a battle if you possess the power you need to ensure victory.

Even if Jesus had backed his divine cause with the power needed to secure its success, this would not have abrogated all human freedom, as some suppose. God need not force compliance by the use of physical violence, by why does he not at least speak out more plainly in his own defense when the cause is threatened? Jesus came to teach us, but God never once raised a hand in Jesus' defense. Isn't it strange behavior for a powerful being to send a frail human into a nearly disastrous situation with no security guards or greater powers to back him up? True, Jesus performed miracles, and this is commonly taken as a sign of his access to divine powers. But when the time came for Jesus to rise to his own defense, why was he so silent? Why were his miracles so little in evidence when he needed them most? Such a non-defensive posture persists right down to the last words of Jesus from the cross, which betray a sense of divine abandonment. To explain God's desertion, theories of the need for an atonement for human sin are invoked. On other occasions God's power to raise Jesus from the dead is pointed to.

Yet mystery still surrounds God's behavior, because God himself never explains these lapses of power and the failure to provide for his defense. It is left to human beings (theologians) to present after-the-fact theories to account for such strange divine behavior. God did not make his purpose perfectly clear, neither in these crucial instances nor in the records left behind. The whole divine salvific plan would be much more convincing if God defended himself and if, for instance, he offered an explicit account of why he tolerated the abuse of Jesus. Why is this tactic of silence in the face of the need for a defense, and then a later mysterious exercise of power in resurrecting the dead, a preferable divine strategy? Certainly Jesus' return to life was not totally convincing to all. Millions today and in every day have been unable to see God's resurrection of Jesus as a totally convincing display of divine power. Surely God could have been more explicit, and less mysterious, had he wanted to be.

Like the argument designed to protect human freedom of the will, theoreticians have given God's apology for him by saying that a non-coercive display leaves room for "faith." Too much direct action on God's part, plus a power display and a dramatic self-defense, might overpower limited human beings and compel belief. That may be true, but even the desire to leave room for human assent (or for denial) does not fully explain God's silence. Moreover, in our world we have not been presented with one divine drama authoritatively translated which we are then free to accept or reject. We have been given at least half a dozen major religious dramas. Each has been interpreted as a divine disclosure, and literally thousands of interpretations are still extant. Such confusion and multiplicity does not protect the human right to free assent. Rather, it often confuses and overpowers us and drives millions into silence because of their inability to deal with such complexity.

Of course, we can and do provide solutions for these dilemmas regarding the inaction of divinity, and these last for a time. Those who satisfactorily explain God's lack of defensive behavior, or who accept the explanations which others offer, become believers in one of the world's theologically based religions. However, there are two problems involved with belief of this kind: (1) The religions of the world remain plural, which leads to "the grass is greener on the other side of the street" tendency. That is, after a time we become unsure and think that believing another religious explanation is preferable. And, (2) since convictions we have once reached can change, this leads to the famous love-hate relationship that exists between the once enthusiastic and the then disappointed lovers and ex-lovers of a particular religion. Problem (1) promotes the vicious infighting that often exists between religious groups. We damn all others and assert the supremacy of the one religion we prefer. Conflict of this kind is a major disgrace in religious history. Problem (2) should convince us that no belief can ever be guaranteed against retraction.

God has not offered us simple alternatives. Rather, the complexity implicit in his action staggers the imagination. In our human fathers we admire clear lines of authority and an exact delineation of the limits of power. Why has God placed us in a less than optimum situation? The human will could decide and pledge itself so much more decisively if only God moved less ambiguously and took action to defend the position he wants us to adopt. Those who believe any religion with conviction, and perhaps with great joy, can do so only if they simplify and overlook a great deal of detail and incredible variety. But for every person who is able to do this, many find themselves confused by a God who will not lay out a clear defense. So his people wander.

The Human Responsibility

God has set us in the midst of a religious drama full of alternatives and fascinating puzzles. However, we could play his game with greater gusto if so many weak creatures were not overwhelmed and lost amid the complexity. So much destruction and venom are spread by religious zealots who try to be absolute in the face of our God-given uncertainties. All religions, every religion, must be pronounced "a mixed bag," even if each may at times rise to great heights and rescue countless individuals in the process. Many spread good works at one moment, only to reverse all this by callous or destructive action in the next instant. Even the most religiously sensitive individual must wonder if God would be better off not to use organized religion as his intermediary and deal directly with human beings in one, clear, consistent, open manner.

Nevertheless, the religious practice and the theology of each religion offer us a justification for their existence through prescribed ritual action, recorded word, and divine symbol. This presents us with a vast and fascinating enterprise—sometimes magnificent, sometimes absurd. The Enlightenment proposal to create a rational religion does not seem to have counted on God's devious ways or his lack of directness, all of which thwarts a clear, final, and single explanation. So the religious story continues, leaving millions to ignore it and millions to explore it. But my particular concern is to see if we can discern some message in God's failure to provide for his own definitive defense. Since men and women act and speak to defend themselves every day, and some do so quite effectively, God must be able to defend himself if he chose to do so. What can this decision not to provide for his own defense mean?

One clear divine message in all this is that if there is to be a defense of God, we humans must provide it. It is odd that what is divine evidently depends for its protection on what is merely human. This situation is a reversal of what many who come to accept a religion think is true. Most who explore a religion seek for a defense against their enemies, both internal and external. The great offer of most widespread religions has always been to grant consolation and solace and assurance. Those who seek out a religion often do so because they feel oppressed by a burden which needs to be lifted or by a mystery which needs to be explained. We come seeking a God to defend us only in the end to find that the nearer we draw to divinity, or the more we explore any religion, the more we find it is we who must offer a defense for God, if he is to have one. If God at all times spoke out with one clear voice, this semi-tragic situation could be avoided. Why do so many seek from religion what is not finally available there? God has not provided a final defense, and the multiplicity of voices raised in his name only underscore his silent inaction.

If we realize all this, it may clarify our understanding of our religious life in at least one respect. *To seek God, to be a follower, means to be ready to defend God at any time and place where divinity comes under attack.* But how can we recognize those special places and times when our defense is called for? And most important, how can we know exactly what action we should take for God's defense in a tense situation? The answers we give depend on our view of God and divinity's demands. Since our visions of God vary, the actions we feel obligated to carry out will vary too. If the uncertainties in the human situation were not as I have described them, a plan of action to defend God could be outlined more definitively. As it is, God seems to have left it to each of us, or at least to those who will take up the battle and who are not preoccupied with other things, to outline his defense. We must each decide where we find God under attack in our day and determine our own defensive strategy on his behalf.

In *The Saviors of God,* Nikos Kazantzakis portrays God as being badly in need of our assistance. Figuratively speaking, according to Kazantzakis, God bleeds, and if we do not rush to assist him in his struggle, all may be lost. This is a challenging view and very modern in its description of God's dramatic need for human help. However, this is not the picture I wish to draw, since I believe Kazantzakis is wrong in attributing failure to God. As God emerges in the issue I have raised over his lack of self-defense, he is a divinity who retains full power to accomplish any task, although the time of its use can be postponed. Nevertheless, so far as the world's history to date is concerned, he has not put an overpowering defense into play against those who attack him, his causes, or his people. God needs our assistance, then, not because he is weak or subject to failure, but because he has refused to lift an arm in his own defense.

The test of human fidelity is that it is left to us to do what God will not do. This is what "faith" or "faithful action" really involves. We need not argue over the meaning of the trinity, although we do need to decide what the nature of divinity is like. What we need to do is to act or to speak out when God's defense is lacking or needed. Somehow our religious fervor has been turned in the wrong direction throughout much of religious history. We spend our energy on arguments over the sacraments, or vestments, or ecclesiastical authority, or buildings, or even over the interpretation of various sacred scriptures and crucial texts. These issues must be dealt with, of course, particularly if they are critical to our understanding of what God demands of us. But it is a gross misplacement of religious effort if we misunderstand our situation over against God. The chief religious questions are: Where are God or his people under attack, and what defense can we offer? This should be our primary concern in any religious life. It is a travesty on the divine intent if, instead, we destroy other human beings in our own rush to achieve security.

God might have provided for his own defense in a painless and non-destructive way. Since he did not choose to do so, to put down or to harm anyone else in the name of God is to do what even God does not do in his own defense. To harm another in the name of religion is always wrong. To say this does not tell us whether violence or force is ever justified in the name of religion, but it does limit the question severely if we see that even God does not use direct force in his own defense. Certainly this means that any action we engage in in the name of religion, whether peaceful or otherwise, must be undertaken on the basis of our own responsibility and as a result of our own decision. In no way can any action we take be argued as directly authorized by God, since he has not even provided a defense of his own. The actions we perform in the name of religion would be better if each were argued for on the basis of individual responsibility and decision—not as if the actions were God's own choices. It is true that divinity's defenseless pose means that we are left to act in God's name. But we must be careful to say that it is our decision to act in any way we elect to defend God and is never his direct command.

All this does argue for a certain gentleness and non-coercive quality in the divine nature, I believe. No matter how destructive the consequences, a tyrannical God surely would not hesitate to use force whenever necessary. The phrase we use against opinionated individuals when we say that they "play God" is a misunderstanding. As it turns out, it is actually the reverse. God seldom issues ultimatums, and he does not try to coerce our every action. He fails to provide for his own defense and leaves that task to individual or group discernment. All this indicates that God seldom issues direct orders to human beings, although perhaps he does to the stars and planets. Just as our own non-violence and non-assertive qualities sometimes permit injustice to be done and destruction to take over because we are too reticent or too permissive, so the gentle and nondirective quality we discern in the divine has its disastrous side effects too, as when men run amuck and are not restrained.

The great issue and mystery in all this is: Has and will this non-defensive posture on God's part continue to be his silent form of behavior to eternity? Or, might he reverse himself at some future time and bring his defensive powers into play? The answer each of us gives to this question will depend on our view of God and the religious story we each listen to. Some theologies picture God as incapable of such a reversal or expenditure of power. But the mystery involved in the defense of God stems from the conviction that he does have the power to enforce his will and yet allows himself to remain indefinitely defenseless. ("How long, oh Lord, how long.") Nothing in our present experience, or at the least very little numerically considered, gives us a basis to predict that God will act differently than he does at present. However, much of our religious conviction rests on an assurance that he will do so after all, on "one fine day."

The Future of God

If we believe that God will reverse his self-restraint some day and bring his power into play to achieve his announced goals, we must use the future as a key to interpret both past and present. We cannot use the past for a touchstone, as those engrossed in the historical quest would have us do, or the present as the empirically-minded advocate. But how is it possible to do that, that is, to use the not-yet-here as a basis for expecting God to act differently than he now does? The future is not present to point to, as an empiricist might wish it were, nor can we compile exact evidence of its direction, as historians would have us do. Yet much religion (particularly Christianity) is based more on an expectation about the future than on a certainty in the past or present. That is one reason "the historical quest" in religion has been so little able to succeed. It begins on a basis different from that projected by the religious message itself. Occasionally we have some piece of present evidence, for example, a miracle, a passage of scripture, or a conversion experience. But these infrequent events are not enough to outbalance the bulk of our present experience in which the majority of humanity remains in bondage and subject to destruction.

God's "eye is on the sparrow," a popular song tells us. But any God who would leave himself presently defenseless must have his eye on the future more than on either the present or the past. His memory may be long and his perception omniscient, but the divine nature must be dominated by the future mode. That is, God depends more on what he will and can do than on what he has done or presently enacts. The tale of creation may begin the biblical documents, but to use Genesis as a foundation to interpret God is to miss the major drama. We need not worry over whether we should teach our children about God as the creator of the world (whatever time and means he employs to accomplish this), but we should teach them about the future of God. The past is history; the present is fact; but the future is where the whole drama of religion is yet to be played out. Those who thought God was dead, because they could not find him operating in history, were partially right. They just did not look for divinity in its right location, even though for a century or two many did think he would eventually be located in history if only we could chart its course "scientifically."

Those who insist on using the evidence of history can never go beyond a marginal belief in the promises of religion. Black slaves persevered and built what is perhaps America's strongest religious spirit. They did not do this based on either their present situation or their past, but on the assumption that God would reverse the course of history for them "some day." The confidence expressed in Negro spirituals is based on future expectations. This is a quite different religious outlook from Teilhard de Chardin, who sees the whole course of the universe directed heavenward. Thus, anyone not inclined to view the course of history romantically will find God defenseless. If so, God's future direction will not be discernible now. Only a radically reconstructed future could do much to rescue the religious promises which we continue to believe even against all present evidence. No matter what words about the future intentions of God that the religious believer clings to, God will have to act differently in the future than he has in the present or in the past if he is to be justified.

The Freedom of God

If the defense of God is as important as I suggest, why haven't philosophers and theologians urged it on us before this? The answer, of course, is that most views of God do not require it. Plato's God is persuasive against chaos but is not involved in deflecting the world from its present course. If you like the present action of God and think it adequate, there is no need for a divine defense. Aristotle's unmoved mover has a key position in the universe, but he does not concern himself with human affairs or with our anguish. Augustine and Thomas Aquinas, Luther and Calvin, each have changeless Gods who have directed the world's final outcome from eternity. But "freedom" is the major social problem today, whether for persons or for Gods. Human volition makes the future less predictable than the social sciences hoped for at their inception, and our freedom is such that the future can never be determined by the past. In the modern world, it is Hegel who gave us the notion that reality could only be understood as "process," but he is also first among those who thought the end could be discerned by charting a dialectic that moved out of the past.

Instead, the past seems to roll on and crush many human religious hopes. This does not always happen, but all too often it does. Our world does not demonstrate that it will achieve any purpose— at any rate certainly not a religious one—given its present course. Therefore, as disillusionment has set in over the Enlightenment hope to build its own new world, our ability to rely on God's future action once again has become crucial. Since history does not reveal the divine intent, we are thrown forward to the future. Along with this comes our realization of God's lack of defense. The modern world perfected the physical sciences at the same time that our insecurity in the world has increased rather than been eliminated, which is not what the social sciences hoped would happen. We are less secure and more alone now, psychiatrists tell us, than at any time in human history. Some want God to provide their lost security, but they do not realize that God himself has chosen not to live in that invulnerable way. As our defenses have broken down and neither psychiatry nor the new social sciences have been able to provide our desired security, the defense of God appears necessary in ways it never did before.

If we must change our vision of God away from what it has been, can we ever say that any action we engage in is "the will of God?" We can, but we must be careful to qualify our meaning, as those who destroy others in the name of God seldom do. No specific action can as such be called "God's will." All that God has willed, and all that we can claim by way of support for any action, is that we act in his defense. How we act, what we do, and the way we decide to carry out our actions—all this is of our choosing and not God's. So it is we who must bear the responsibility and we who will be evaluated on the basis of our choices. These decisions are our share of the responsibility as we work to establish a new order; God has given that project to us. It is for God to demand defense; it is for us to choose a specific course of action and accept responsibility for doing so. God will accept responsibility for having urged us to act in defense of his causes, but not for the specific means and the particular actions we engage in on his behalf.

If this is so, can we ever claim that God speaks directly to us? Many individuals assert, as a justification of their behavior, that God has done so. People often claim to act on specific instructions from God. Although it is not characteristic of Jesus, the biblical record abounds in stories of those instructed in specifics by God. I believe God may very well speak directly. But the interpretation of what we hear, how we translate God's word into action, and even our claim to have heard him, for all that we must bear responsibility. This is particularly true due to the many conflicting reports we have about what God's direct instructions are. We know human beings can be deluded. Our decision that one divine set of instructions is authentic and another pseudo, this is entirely up to us. God's instructions appear in many places and on many lips, but none bears an official seal of guaranteed source. From out of the conflicting voices that come to us, it is our responsibility to say: This is from God; this is not. He has not yet broken his silence to confirm who has heard him correctly and who has grossly misinterpreted him. Such disclosure is for a future drama. It should be an interesting scene when it is played out with God in the lead role.

Is It Possible to Achieve Unity in the Defense of God?

When we speak about "the defense of God," can those among us who follow nontheistic religions make any sense of this? To support any religious way is to protect and to uphold some values, goals, and forms of life which are not highly prized in the everyday world. Were this not so, if some did not persevere along uncommon paths, religion would be unnecessary in society or in the lives of human beings. All religions, whether theistic or nontheistic, are called to a divine defense. That means: to protect, to uphold, and to follow pathways which might otherwise be trampled under foot or forgotten by the secular multitude. To return to theistic language for a moment, how odd of God not to establish clearly for us what is valued divinely so that secular society could recognize these as obvious values too. After all, the world could have been designed as one large co-ed monastery with all of us seeking God in community. But this is not the plan of things as we find it around us, except as pictured in some romantic religious visions.

No religion has a one hundred percent following among the

peoples of the world. Thus, we face the need for internal campaigns to restore purity among the faithful, and we also hear about the need to drive out the infidels. Ironically, religious wars and intolerance and persecution come from the same source that drives us to the defense of God. Any religious goal is fragile. We realize how easily its aims can be perverted. Thus, we ought to defend our particular religious goal with all our energy. But in our attempt to do this we too often go astray and turn instead to destroy or to decry all who do not share our particular goal. Rage fails to distinguish between those who are antithetical to all religious ways and those who simply hold differently formed religious aims. All those who are religiously oriented (which is not everyone) should unite—theist and nontheist alike—in a non-tyrannical defense of those values the natural world is not attuned to. As we pursue these various plans to defend the sacred, we should pledge neither to destroy nor to denounce those whose religious visions differ from our own.

Quite obviously, if any program could count on receiving majority support, it would need no special defense. However, we know religion will always be the concern of a minority. True, in certain societies and at certain times one religious form or another often ascends to a majority position and dominates by political connection. Then, carried away by victory, that religious form may assume that religious forces should dominate in the secular domain. However, the history of religions shows us that triumphant and dominant religions tend to spoil and corrupt. When ecclesiastics control power, they become prey to power seekers just as kings do. When this happens, the religious consciousness of mankind, which is connected to a thirst for purity, rebels and strives to construct new religious forms. Then an age of new religious movements is launched, just as we have witnessed recently. But this continual tendency toward heresy, that is, to depart from the reigning orthodoxies, is never welcomed by the religious establishment. Too much is at stake, including the carefully cultivated religious security of dominant groups, for them to react calmly to the threat posed by new groups who form and drain away adherents.

Not every new religious movement is true and pure and good. Nor can any group or leader be all good, I believe, whether religious or political. But religious groups spring up in response to needs not being met by the already established religions. Of course, movements may be born partly out of the sense that although religious celebrations are carried on, God has been abandoned or left defenseless once again. The majority in any society hear other voices besides angels calling them. But those who are religiously sensitive should awaken whenever what they perceive to be God's goals are neglected. They should respond by issuing a call to his defense. All of us can answer to this alarm to salvage religious aims and goals from threatened prostitution, no matter what our religious orientation may be, theist and nontheist alike. To attempt to reconcile all theologies and their differences is another matter. Intellectual differences are important but still are a secondary concern. The practical issue is that we must not allow genuine religious life, no matter what its form, to be stamped out or lost by the lure of the secular world.

The Religious Manifesto

In the *Communist Manifesto*, Karl Marx and Frederick Engels issued a call to the workers of the world to unite. In rebelling you have nothing to lose but your chains, the authors told them. They thought that all workers would arise and form a worldwide community that bridged nationality and race. In this way workers could free themselves from provincial concerns and lead a worldwide revolution to the benefit of all humanity. This call has had worldwide repercussions—some liberating, some destructive. In any case, the vision Marx and Engels held out, that is, to form a classless society based on a growing international community of workers, has not materialized. Realizing that corrupting forces and vested power structures would oppose this projected internationalism, Marx and Engels argued for the necessity to use violence, as the only means strong enough to overcome existing barriers to human unity. Violence can tear down existing structures, but today we have come to think that violence may also defeat the rise of the just society it seeks. In any case, I believe violence of any sort is unacceptable in defense of religious goals. Since the goals of religious life are so fragile that violence is sure to destroy the aim, they should pledge an abstinence from all wars.

Religious life needs to be defended from attack from those within as well as from those without, as Kierkegaard noted. Unfortunately, too much energy is expended within religious groups opposing those with whom they disagree religiously. Thus, those who rally to our call to defend both God and the goals of religion from secular attack know that they face opposition from friends as well as from enemies. Can we agree that religious ways are plural, that adherence to doctrine is not our main goal, but that the preservation of religious ways of life against their extinction is? If so, we can respond to a call for the defense of God on a worldwide scale. In doing so we know that we rise above race and class and nature, just as Marx projected for his society. If we take the pledge to abstain from violence, however, we also know that we will never revolutionize the world's political and economic structures. Marx is right that such institutions both use and breed violence. Only a God whose whole being moves toward the future can achieve social change that is final and definite. Still, God needs our defense in the present hour against all attacks on that expected future which is yet to come.

All over the world religious life exists under the threat of destruction. God has taken a vow of silence. He has no voice or arms to defend himself but ours. Religious workers of the world, cease your age-old rivalries and internal strife; unite, arise. Defend the divine traditions in every land.

2

God in His Own Defense?: And/ Or in Defense of Humankind

ADRIO KÖNIG

The title of this paper is a critical question directed at the subject under discussion: the defense of God. The main themes of this paper are summarized as follows:

1. We are not called upon to defend God.
2. As to whether God defends himself, the answer is both yes and no, depending on the angle from which one views the biblical message.
3. The crux of the biblical message is that God defends humanity.
4. First, however, we need to ask: Who is the God in question?

The Exclusiveness of the God of the Bible

In this discussion about the defense of God, I must state pertinently that my point of departure is not a universal God who is merely perceived and venerated differently by the various religions. Nor do I assume that those theistic philosophies which postulate an Absolute or Ultimate or Ground of Being are simply referring in their own terms to the God of Israel. I assume, on the contrary, that there is not only a clear distinction but even a tension between the God of Israel and other Gods. Israel accepted the exclusiveness and intolerance of their God. Whether speaking of the Canaanite Gods or of those of Egypt, Babylon or Greece, the Bible's preponderant message always is that these are different Gods and, compared to the God of Israel, not even real Gods.

Yahweh is the only true God. This is why the concept of repentance is so prominent in the appeal to the worshippers of other Gods to turn to God, the Father of Jesus Christ. Obviously this exclusiveness of Yahweh creates peculiar problems for an open discussion about God. However, it enhances the value of the discussion if these problems are faced up to, and not ignored in a bid to facilitate the conversation. I am in fact convinced that Jewish and Christian theologians who simply accept that the God of the Bible and the Gods of other religions are one and the same are over-emphasizing subsidiary strands of the biblical message at the expense of its powerful emphasis on the exclusiveness of God.[1] To exclude this uniqueness and exclusiveness of Israel's God from an open discussion and to place all Gods on the same level may indeed simplify matters; but it means that at the crucial point the God of Israel is not presented in the way that Israel and the apostles understood him.

In Defense of God?

It is true that the concept of God held by certain systems makes it essential to try and prove God's existence. Certainly such proofs are more important in philosophical systems than in religions and in world views. Philosophical systems are often concerned with total reality and with the interrelatedness of all things. The following questions then have obvious importance: Where do all things come from? Is everything meaningful? Does it have a purpose? And these questions inevitably raise further questions as to an Absolute Being.

However, philosophical proofs of God's existence form a sharp contrast with the seeming lack of any attempt at such proof in the Bible. The Bible's proofs are of a certain kind. They are proofs presented by God himself to prove himself against other Gods. The biblical writers make no attempt to submit theoretical proofs that there is a God, that the God of Israel really exists, or that he is a God of justice (theodicy).

This difference between philosophers and theologians who try to prove God's existence and biblical authors who attempt no such thing may have more than one explanation. For instance, there is a profound difference between the world of the men who wrote the Bible and the modern post-Enlightenment world of the West. To the writers of the Bible, the existence of God required no proof. In the world of biblical times the term "God" did not represent an exclusive concept but rather a generic concept such as "man" or "dog." There were many Gods: the problem was their relationship to one another. Some religions, such as that of early Egypt, showed a strong tendency to link up certain Gods and combine them into a single entity; hence the double names of many Egyptian Gods.

Other religions stressed the question of which was the strongest God or Gods—hence the conflict between the Gods, as in Babylon. But the lesser Gods were still recognized as Gods.

In the religion of Israel and of the Christians, however, the question is: Who is the *true* God?—with the implication that only he can really be thought of as God. Therefore God's "self-proofs" in the Bible are in no sense intended as proof of his existence; this would be absurd in terms of the religion of Israel or of any people of that time. His self-proofs are intended to prove that only he is truly God, the only true God, because only he can do what a God is expected to do (e.g., Ps. 82, Isa. 40–55).[2]

By contrast, the post-Enlightenment Westerner lives in a world where the existence of God is no longer self-evident, where many thinkers in fact question why man should believe in a God at all. The situational difference may therefore help to explain why no proof of God's existence was needed in biblical times, whereas some philosophies and theologies of modern times are preoccupied with proofs of this kind.

But this is not the whole story nor indeed the most important part of it. There is an even more fundamental difference between the Western philosophies and the message of the Bible, a difference that makes proofs of God's existence redundant and even undesirable in biblical terms. Israel experienced God as a *personal* God, a *covenant* God who *related* to his people and to humanity as a whole, who by this relationship imparted a specific character to *history* and became increasingly *known* to Israel. These few basic points imply a decisive structural difference from most philosophical (and even some theological) systems of thought, in which God is in principle approached as a problem and mainly described in impersonal terms that tend to turn God into an object.

Philosophers feel the need to reflect on reality and to determine whether reality provides reasons for accepting the existence of a supernatural being above or behind reality. To them it is an *open* situation in which humanity has to find a way by means of intellect. But in the Bible we encounter a *given* situation in which humanity reacts to the initiatives of that God who already related to people and so became known to them. Structurally, then, proofs of God are not only redundant but even meaningless, in terms of the biblical approach to God, whereas in most philosophical systems they are indispensable. This means that Jewish and Christian theologians should have serious reservations as to the compatibility of proofs of God with the nature of the God they are concerned with: the *known, personal, covenant* God.

It is remarkable, too, how a foreign image of the biblical God has been created by traditional theological and philosophical proofs. Compare those abstract concepts of being (*Seinsbegriffe*) with the living, involved, responsive God of the Bible. It is a moot point whether an unbeliever persuaded by the usual proofs would have become convinced of the existence of the God of Israel, and not merely of some intellectual abstraction or logical necessity quite unrelated to Israel's God of the covenant, the Father of Jesus who delivers and preserves.

It seems possible, by and large, that proofs of God in the Jewish and Christian traditions have been counterproductive, creating a false image of the God of the Bible. In the actual religious life of the church members and in missionary situations, it is significant that such proofs have never played an important part.

God in His Own Defense[?]

The question mark in brackets is meant to signify that the question as to whether God defends himself may be answered both positively and negatively, depending on the perspective. Certainly, the only proofs of God in the Bible are self-proofs: actions of God in history that prove to men and women that he is the only true God. In specific biblical traditions these self-proofs in fact play a vital part; for example, in Deutero-Isaiah and in the apostles' proclamation of the resurrection and second coming of Jesus Christ.

Apparently, however, there is also a defenselessness about God's actions that makes it possible not to believe in him—most clearly demonstrated, perhaps, in the actions of Jesus, particularly in his rejection by the Jews and his crucifixion. This defenselessness may indicate that in his self-proofs God is concerned not so much with his own defense as with the defense of humankind. We now proceed to examine first the self-proofs of God and then the defenselessness of God.

The Bible might well be called the book of the proofs of God—his self-proofs of which his people are no more than the mouthpiece. God displays these self-proofs in his history with Israel and the world, and Israel—and the Christians—are called to testify to this, and in the process to glorify him and to invite all people to believe in him.

Unlike the traditional proofs of God, the biblical proofs therefore are historical proofs—actions of God in his dealings with Israel and the world that have had a decisive effect on the course of history. These historical proofs of God are related to the basic structure of the most important biblical traditions. It is a historical structure, including narratives, stories, proclamations and praises referring to events, and deeds done by Yahweh or still to be done by him. The Bible is a book of history and not of philosophy, a book that relates and not a book that reasons.

The main reason for this is the way in which the people of Israel experienced their relationship with God. God revealed himself not in abstract ways but in history. Their basic and determinative experience with God was the historical exodus from Egypt; but this was not merely incidental. Their entire subsequent relationship with God is a historical one. Their God is also the God of their fathers, of Abraham, Isaac, and Jacob; moreover, he is the God who created heaven and earth. Right from the beginning history developed under his guidance. But that was indeed only the beginning. He is also the God of David, the God of the exile and return; to the Christians he is more particularly the Father of Jesus Christ, the God who justifies sinners and raises the dead—hence the God of hope. All of history relates to God. He is above all a historical God, a God whose heart is with humankind.

All this demonstrates afresh how inappropriate the abstract concepts of the traditional proofs of God are in relation to the God of Israel. We simply cannot speak of God appropriately in Thomas's terms—first and unmoved mover, first effective and efficient cause, the one self-sufficient being, the highest good and perfect intelligence. Some of these concepts may indeed be given a biblical content, but the Bible expresses its faith in downright historical terms: Creator, God of the covenant, Father, Savior, Renewer.

It would be untrue to say that because of the self-proofs of God, the Bible—unlike the philosophical proofs of God—does not require us to *reflect on God*. On the contrary, the biblical authors think and speak of God a great deal, but in a different way. In philosophy we have an open situation to which the thinker has to impart structure and content if he can. Is there a God? What is he like? What does he do? How can he be known? But the Bible presents us with a given situation: God is known, he is the covenant God, the God who is on the way, the God who cares about and is involved with his creation. Much reflection is needed on this given reality;

much debate about its meaning is required. But God is revealed, known, involved. And therefore it is testimony, not reflection, that is paramount. Israel—and Christendom later on—is enjoined to tell his story.

A great statesman proves himself by his competent statecraft, while the news media simply report his actions, explain their significance—and everyone comes to revere him more and more. In the same way, God proves himself by his historical actions, while his followers play the part of the news media by publicizing his deeds. The Bible is not so much a philosophical text as a newspaper.

Before we proceed to a closer examination of a number of the biblical proofs of God, another striking feature of these proofs claims our attention: the fact that they convince people by bringing them to believe in God in such a way that they surrender their lives to him. Once again we should realize that this God who proves himself is a specific God. Whoever is convinced by God's self-proofs that he is the true God is not convinced merely of the existence of a "Deity" or a "Supreme Being" or an "Ultimate," but of the God of Israel, the Father of Jesus, the God who enters into a covenant with humankind—the God who is our God and calls us to be his people.

An uninvolved acceptance of the uninvolved existence of Israel's God is therefore impossible, because he is in his very essence the God of the covenant. One only really accepts *him* if one accepts him as one's *own* God and accepts oneself as his child. Faith is confidence, surrender, and obedience, and for this reason faith is the prerequisite for a knowledge of God. As E. Jüngel said, proof of God independent of our faith is impossible *for our sakes* because it would leave us uninvolved and therefore unredeemed; it would not bind us to the God of the covenant. Luther called faith the creator of God—not in the sense that faith calls God into existence, but in the sense that faith brings him into our lives. The self-proofs of God must therefore be accepted in faith if they are to speak to us at all.

A warning is needed here against the misunderstanding that this emphasis on faith really amounts to a pious fraud. So far we have stressed the self-proofs of God and questioned theoretical proofs as unnecessary and even inappropriate. Now it may seem that the inherent value of these self-proofs is being drastically relativized by making them dependent on our contribution: faith. It may seem as though the inadequacy of God's self-proofs has to be supplemented by our faith.

But this is indeed a misunderstanding. The necessity of our faith does not arise from the limited persuasive value of God's self-proofs. Our faith is simply the only appropriate response to God's self-proofs. Because he is who he is (our God, our Creator, the Lord of our lives) and because we are what we are (his creatures, his covenant partners), there can in principle be no recognition of God *as he is* without surrender, involvement, and obedience to him. This is what makes the traditional philosophical proofs of God so inappropriate. They abstract the existence of God from his essential being as an *involved* God. The "mere existence" of God cannot be proved because there is no such thing. Israel's God is a specific God; the God who is present in relationships, the Father of Jesus (our Saviour), who lays claim to our lives.

The Self-Proofs of God

Faith is not "help" which we give to God's self-proofs because they are unconvincing in themselves. Their power to convince is an inherent one. But we need to examine this point more closely.

To start, consider three of God's self-proofs: the exodus from Egypt, the Babylonian exile, and the return from Babylon. No other event in the Old Testament is as decisive as the exodus. It is the foundation of Israel's identity as the people of God. Time after time, and in every conceivable context, the Bible refers to the exodus. Obviously, theologians have been asking critical questions about the date and circumstances of the exodus, and there are differences of opinion on many points. Yet the story has certain striking features that make it more feasible to accept that this was indeed the doing of Yahweh than that it was the doing of some other God, or mere coincidence. H. H. Rowley has dealt with a number of these features.[3] First of all there is the fact that the God who led the people out of Egypt had apparently not been served by them previously, except perhaps in a very sporadic way. (Cf. Exod. 3:6, 15, 16, where the Lord repeatedly tells Moses who he is, and Exod. 3:13 which assumes that Moses would have to explain to the people who had sent him to them.) The covenant that was entered into at Sinai, and the giving of the laws and expressions such as Exodus 6:25–6, indicate that during the exodus a new relationship between the Lord and the people came into existence, and that before the exodus the people do not appear to have regarded themselves as the people of the Lord. Had Israel later on invented

21

the story of the exodus, they would have made familiar Gods, and not a new God, responsible for it. And if Moses had gone to them of his own accord (and had accordingly not met the Lord at the burning bush—Exod. 3), he would not have gone in the name of a relatively unknown God because of the possibility that they would not acknowledge that God.

Then there is the fact that they made no military contribution to their liberation from the powerful Egyptian Pharaoh. The Lord compelled the Pharaoh by means of plagues to let them go, and at the Red Sea, it was only the Lord who delivered them. From their side, they contributed nothing. Were the story invented, the people would never have missed such an opportunity to laud their military achievements. In such a case, Moses would have been portrayed as a military leader who had whipped up the people's courage to great acts of heroism. But this element is entirely lacking in the story. Moses acts as a prophet and not as a military leader. He came only to announce to the people what the Lord would do to deliver them. Rowley mentions many further features in the story which make it more reasonable to accept than to reject Israel's claim that Yahweh led them out of Egypt. In fact the thrust of the exodus story is a reflection on the courage and initiative of the Israelites—and a people would hardly invent such a story about its origins unless it had a strong historical basis.[4]

In the other two focal events of the Old Testament, the exile and the return from exile, God proves himself in different ways. First, the exile. We have already referred to the remarkable fact that the God who led Israel out of Egypt was at that stage relatively strange and unfamiliar to them. No people would arbitrarily invent the story that a new, unknown God had decreed their nationhood. That is why this fact enhances the story's credibility, especially the fact of Yahweh's guidance. In the exile, however, it is to some extent the other way around. By this time a firm relationship had existed for centuries between Israel and their God. The Old Testament makes it clear that God—like other Gods in the countries surrounding Israel—cared for his people. What is shockingly new, however, is that this God, Israel's *own* God, would send his own people into a devastating exile. This was unheard of in Israel and among the surrounding peoples, and it was a particular humiliation for Israel. Once again, it is unlikely that the prophets would have fabricated this. As we have said, no people will arbitrarily evolve a negative picture of themselves or of their own history.[5] The credibility of the idea that the exile was *God's* judgment on Israel is heightened by the fact that several prophets had announced it *beforehand*: this is perfectly clear from the dating of the work of prophets such as Amos and Isaiah.

This phenomenon of proclamation-in-advance plays an even more crucial role in the return from exile. Serious problems of faith had developed while the people were in exile. Several generations were born in exile, and eventually they began to question whether the exile itself and its long duration were not a proof that their God was less powerful than the Babylonian Gods.

Into this situation came an unknown prophet to proclaim the incomparable greatness of God. The other Gods did not even merit the name of "God"—they were no-gods, "nothings" (Isa. 41:24, 29 NEB). In contrast, God proved himself in two ways: he could explain what had already happened (the exile) *and* proclaim what was still to come—exactly the two things the prophet demanded of the other divinities and which they could not do (Isa. 41:21–29).

God's proclamation of the future is, of course, much more than mere prediction. He *brings about* what is to happen to Babylon and its people. He "calls" Cyrus the Persian to conquer Babylon and permit the Jews to return to Jerusalem (e.g., Isa. 46-9–13). Clearly, then, he is able to intervene decisively in the future.

As we have already noted, this proclamation-in-advance plays a particularly important part in the return from exile. It is more than mere prediction, which could have come true by chance. It involves, in fact, a decisive turn in history. God changes the course of history to conform to his purpose with it. This is why his involvement in history is not restricted to an incident here and there. As von Rad has pointed out, it is to Israel that we owe the concept of history. They saw their own history—and, to an increasing extent, world history—as events taking place under God's guidance and serving his purposes.

The books of the prophets contain convincing evidence that these announcements of what was to befall the Jews (the exile and the return) were in fact made before the events themselves took place. I have already referred to the dates assigned to prophetic writings such as Amos, Jeremiah, and Isaiah, who indeed prophesied long before the exile. Deutero-Isaiah presents another enlightening example of a prophecy uttered before the event, thus contributing to the credibility of the prophet's message. In Isaiah 46:1–2 we read how the Gods of Babylon would collapse and be loaded onto wagons and carted away when Cyrus captured Babylon. The point of the prophet's message emerges in verse 3 ff., where he glorifies Yahweh, who would help his people in their need; whereas the Gods of Babylon would be helpless to defend themselves against Cyrus, and their worshippers would have to come to their aid.

However, when Babylon was subsequently captured by Cyrus, he did not interfere with the Babylonian religion: the Gods were not removed from the temples and loaded onto wagons as described in Isaiah 46. It is obvious, therefore, that if Deutero-Isaiah had been writing after the fall of Babylon, he would not have used such images to portray the fall of these Gods.

The resurrection of Jesus Christ is, of course, the cardinal proof of God. Owing to lack of space, however, it must suffice to refer to the work of W. Pannenberg and others and to offer two brief but important remarks.

Is the resurrection of Jesus really a proof of God? If one accepts the eschatological interpretation, it is indeed. This interpretation is challenged, however, by the fact that the final resurrection which began with that of Jesus has not yet been completed. It is therefore a proof of God that is open to the future and hence, in this sense, has limited powers of persuasion.

There is, however, another sense in which Jesus' resurrection is a self-proof of God. The thing that makes God God—according to specific Old Testament traditions—is his concern for the poor and oppressed and those who have no rights. Jesus displayed this "downward" orientation in a remarkable way—identification with the poor, the rejected, the unacceptable. By raising him from the dead, God identified himself with Jesus and therefore with his "downward" identification.

The Defenselessness of God

If it is true that God's historical self-proofs have been neglected in Christian theology, it is true also that God's omnipotence has been given a one-sided emphasis at the expense of what we have called his defenselessness.[6] At a superficial glance, the defenselessness of God might seem to contradict his self-proofs. The next few pages will be devoted to an examination of this point.

One could approach the defenselessness of God by dealing in the first place with the *nature* of God's self-proofs (and his actions in general), then with the *limited* effect of his self-proofs, and finally with *possible explanations* of this limited effort.

As regards the *nature* of God's self-proofs, it is possible that a change has come about in this respect, particularly in terms of the actions of Jesus. The Old Testament puts great emphasis on God's forceful demonstrations of power. The Egyptians are forced against their will to let the Israelites go, and Canaan is given to Israel by force. The person who may well represent the climax of Israel's history (David) achieves his position by military power. God has no favorites, of course—he uses force against his own people too, as strikingly illustrated in the two exiles. But the principle is upheld fairly consistently, including the return from exile and even up to the book of Revelation. God's forceful demonstrations of power play a conspicuous part. The Creation is a classic example, particularly the portrayal of God's victory over the forces of chaos.

But the coming of Jesus Christ introduces another aspect of the action of God. Jesus does not use force as God did in the Old Testament. He achieves his purpose not by military might but, among other ways, by accepting crucifixion (a shameful death) and by his resurrection. After his resurrection he appears only to his followers; he therefore did not even make direct use of the resurrection to bring unbelieving people to faith in him. Since that time he has worked through the Holy Spirit, who uses spiritual persuasion and shows no trace of the Old Testament display of coercive power. If one accepts a concept of God that is characterized by the use of coercive force, this type of behavior would have to be described as powerlessness.

The question is, however, whether a more spiritual method directed at inward persuasion is necessarily inappropriate to God. It might, in the final analysis, prove to be more appropriate and even more effective. The church's worldwide missionary expansion has certainly, in the long run, meant more to the world than the military conquest of Canaan.

God's defenselessness has another aspect, however: its limited effect on mankind. I have deliberately not described it as an *absence of effect,* because this would be far from true. In fact the entire history of the Western world has been decisively influenced by the history of Israel and the gospel of Jesus Christ.[7]

Despite massive contributions to the humanization of society, one is constantly brought up short, in the history of Israel and of the church, by the *limited* effect of God's self-proofs. Historically it is a fact that these self-proofs have not convinced all of humankind—in many cases not even the majority within nations which have a strong Christian component. It is doubtful how many of the peoples of the world in Old Testament times had even heard of Israel's God and his marvelous deeds—even those nations who lived in close proximity with Israel. Deutero-Isaiah, the prophet most concerned with the self-proofs of God, is largely addressing Israel itself in an effort to change their doubt and despair by inspiring new faith and confidence in the Lord.

Important traditions in the Bible indeed look forward to a universal response to the mighty deeds of God. At various stages of Israel's history, there were prophets who looked expectantly to a future when all the nations would flock to Jerusalem to submit to Israel's God (Gen. 12:2; 22:18; Isa. 2; 66: 17–24; Mic. 4; Jer. 3:7; Zech. 8:20 ff.). Jesus, after his resurrection, sent the disciples out to make disciples of *all* the nations (Matt. 28:19); and Luke, in the variety of peoples present in Jerusalem at the outpouring of the Holy Spirit, appears to see the fulfillment (or at least a provisional fulfillment) of the prophets' expectations. We find this perspective, the whole world on its knees before God, throughout the New Testament (as in 1 Cor. 15:25–28; Eph. 1:10; Phil. 2:10–11; Col. 3:11; Rev. 5:9–14, especially the tremendous emphasis in v. 13).

Notwithstanding the effect the deeds of God have had on humanity, and notwithstanding the expectation of a future universal victory of God over all peoples, it still remains true that up to now God's works have had a limited effect.

In this context it may be useful to look in passing at two points of interest: Israel's unfaithfulness to God, and the reaction to the miracles and general conduct of Jesus. The history of Israel produces constant examples of infidelity to God. Even the very beginning of human history is blighted by the same evil omen (Adam and Eve). The most blatant examples of Israel's unfaithfulness are the periods preceding the exiles and the eventual rejection of Jesus the Messiah. Israel's unfaithfulness and defection to other Gods are made even more appalling by the Bible's insistence on the uniqueness of Israel's God. He is the only true God, the God who cares and provides. The prophet Jeremiah even ascribes an exclamation of surprise at Israel's unfaithfulness to God himself: "And so I command the sky to shake with horror, to be amazed and astonished" (Jer. 2:12). Why does the history of Israel—the history of the only true God and his chosen people—end in Israel rejecting her Messiah and thereby rejecting her God?

The limited effect of Jesus' ministry is even more striking. Of course, occasions are mentioned, especially by Luke, when his ministry was powerful and convincing. The crowds were filled with wonder at his authoritative actions; again and again they gave glory to God for his deeds of power—responding to his teaching but more particularly to his miracles, especially the exorcisms.[8] And again and again, because of these acts, numerous groups are convinced of his claim to divinity and believe in him.[9] But in the end Jesus' ministry is a "failure." He is rejected by the majority of *his own people,* even crucified—a shamefully humiliating death, particularly for a Jew—at the insistence of the people, incited by their religious leaders. Moreover, Jesus in no way resisted the cross or even tried to achieve the victory for which his followers had hoped. He accepted the cross and would not save himself by a further act of power, even though he was challenged to do so by people who promised to believe in him if he did!

Although in the first few centuries the Christians, in the power of the glorified Christ manifested through the Holy Spirit, had a powerful impact in the Mediterranean countries, the general impression of the history of the church over the past two millennia is not that of a success story. There were indeed times when a large and influential part of the human race was convinced by God's self-proofs; but there were also times (such as our own) when this could only be said of a rather small minority of the human race. In addition, the remarkable lifestyle of Jesus has generally had a very limited influence on the lifestyles of even his own followers. Thus we have more than a few examples of the limited effect of the deeds of God in human history.

It is obviously important to reflect on *possible explanations* of this limited impact of the self-proofs of God. A number of possibilities present themselves, such as the unfaithfulness of his followers and the sinful resistance of humankind to God's inclination to help the underdog.

Although this paper rejects the notion that we need to prove or defend God, it would be a mistake to imagine that humans—in this case the people of God—do not have any responsibility. On the contrary—to develop a metaphor used earlier on—the mass media have the power to silence a remarkable person or to nullify the effects of an event by ignoring them. God's people of the Old Testament were "reporters" who had the responsibility of showing forth his power and glory to the surrounding nations. And since Christ, the church has had the duty of literally going out as his ambassadors to present him to all nations.

On the whole, Israel failed in this mission—particularly in light of how God's purposes are represented by certain Old Testament traditions. According to these, God's intention was to bless the whole earth through Israel (Abraham), as in Gen. 12:2 and 22:18. If the people were faithful, he would bless and prosper them so that the surrounding nations would be convinced that Israel's God was the true God. And this would bring the nations flocking to Jerusalem—the expectation we have already mentioned. In actual fact, however, Israel became increasingly unfaithful, so that God had to repeatedly chastise them and permit the neighboring peoples to subdue them. In the end, in the two great exiles, he had to humiliate them to the dust. The results are obvious. Instead of being attracted to the Lord by the blessed and prosperous life of Israel, the nations mocked him because of the disasters and humiliations that overtook Israel (Isa. 52:5; Ezek. 36:20–21; cf. Num. 14:15–16 and 1 Sam. 4:19–22).

The Christian era, too, has produced numerous examples of cases where the organized church, or Christian groups or individuals, have by their conduct discouraged people from believing in Christ. There are many who see Gandhi's response to Christianity in South Africa as such an example.

In connection with this unfaithfulness and defective witness in the Lord's followers, one needs to note that it does attest to the consistency of God that he is prepared to punish his own people—even at the risk of endangering his self-proofs—rather than hushing up sin "in a good cause."

Another point to examine is the natural resistance of humankind (including God's people) to the implications of his self-proofs. God's orientation is *"downwards"* to the small, the helpless, the deprived, the wicked. One of the objections to God's self-proofs was that they were manifested mainly in the history of Israel—a small and unimportant nation (Deut. 7:7) descended from slaves and without any significant cultural or military achievements, by the standards of the great nations of the time. Within Israel itself, too, at least a part of the nation's infidelity was caused by the Lord's characteristic partiality to the deprived groups in Israel: widows,

orphans, and strangers. God requires justice, and this evokes resistance from influential groups who often owe their position and
prosperity to injustice, especially the exploitation of the deprived. It
is, of course, these groups that dominated the "people of Israel" and
brought about exile by God on account of their unrighteousness.

This same "downward" tendency in Jesus was undoubtedly a
considerable factor in the negative reaction of the religious leaders
and eventually of the people. The Pharisees often rejected Jesus'
friendliness to sinners, whereas we see in this selfsame behavior of
Jesus a striking proof of God—because he is the God who "declares
the guilty to be innocent" (Rom. 11:5EV). The openness of Jesus to
prostitutes, tax collectors, and "the people who do not know the
law" was undoubtedly offensive. But it is offensive because of
man's sinful nature which is fixated on itself and its own group
rather than being directed, like God, toward others and especially
toward the underdog.

The cross is indeed the event in which both man and God are
revealed for what they are. The crucifixion of Jesus was no accident
or surprise; it was the culmination of sinful man's reaction against
the God of justice who cares for the wretched. On the other hand, it
is the form and proof *par excellence* of the love of God. These are the
lengths to which he is prepared to go to achieve his real purpose: the
defense of mankind. Even if it costs him his credibilty in the eyes of
sinful humanity, he still—in Jesus—chooses this extremity of degradation because of his love for that humanity. *In other words, humankind rejects God because of God's love for humankind.* It is this fact that
makes his rejection a proof of his divinity rather than a negation of
it. Thus we come to what really matters to God: not his own
defense but the defense of humankind.

God in the Defense of Humankind

Toward the end of the previous section particularly, a good deal has
been said about this basic objective of God. Because this was said in
a variety of contexts, however, it is necessary to summarize and
illustrate it in somewhat more detail.

God's deepest concern in his self-proofs is with the defense of
humankind. Taken as a whole, the Bible is mainly concerned with
what God does for the sake of man and for his benefit—even at
God's own expense. The second story of creation is already a classic

example of what God does for humankind and of what it costs God himself (Gen. 2–4).

Because there is so much injustice and misery on earth, God's words and deeds are directed more particularly toward those who suffer and are deprived. However, this does not imply that God practices favoritism and does not care for other people as well. In caring for the wretched, he also seeks to liberate those who are responsible for their misery.

It is surely one of the most striking facts in the entire Bible that of all the nations in the ancient Middle East—some of them nations of great culture with almost unlimited possibilities—God chose the groups of Jewish slaves in Egypt (Deut. 7:7ff). And although no reason is given at that point for God's love for them, it becomes clear elsewhere that this love was specifically in response to their inferiority and misery.

Even within Israel, God increasingly distinguishes between the rich and mighty on the one hand and the oppressed and deprived on the other. In fact, God becomes "the God of the widows, orphans and strangers"—the three groups in Israel that had the fewest rights and privileges. Psalm 82:2–4, for example, describes the prime characteristics of a God who claims to be truly God as follows: He must stop judging unjustly; he must no longer be partial to the wicked. He must defend the rights of the poor and the orphans; he must be fair to the needy and the helpless. He must rescue them from the power of evil men.

Because the other Gods do not do exactly these things, they are not true Gods. Israel's God is the one who finds his identity in this fact: *he acts in defense of defenseless human beings.* The climax of this divine tendency comes in the history of Jesus Christ. Because *all* men are guilty before God, and the whole world has incurred his righteous judgment so that it stands defenseless before the righteous God, *God in Jesus gives himself as the defense of the defenseless against his own justice.* Seen in this light, the cross is the foremost proof of God in the Bible. No other God had ever loved humankind like this. This is what reveals God's identity and is why, according to Paul, God is the one "who justifies the wicked" (Rom. 4:5 NEB) or, "who declares the guilty to be innocent" (Rom. 4:5 EV).

In Jesus, God directs his forgiveness at the whole world (John 3:16). There is no natural or ethical limit to his redemption. In fact, the believers form a close-knit community of love drawn from all walks of society (Jews and Greeks, male and female, slaves and free, scholars and barbarians) and from all nations of the world (1 Cor. 12:13; Gal. 3:28; Eph. 2:11–3:6; Col. 3:11; Matt. 28:19).

As we have seen, however, this predisposition of God evokes violent resistance from those who have power and privilege because they too are sinners and absorbed in themselves. This should probably be seen as one of the main reasons why the self-proofs of God have so limited an impact on humankind. It reinforces God's credibility, however, that he is prepared to be rejected by his people if they decline to accept this predisposition of his and to take pity on the helpless.

NOTES

1. It is true that Israel took over concepts from other religions and thereby enriched its own concept of God. See Adrio König, *Here Am I* (Grand Rapids, Mich.: Eerdmans, 1982), 16 ff. But these are subsidiary themes in the Old Testament.

2. This statement must not be misinterpreted to mean that there are objective requirements for Gods to satisfy in order to prove themselves Gods. Some Greek philosophers did indeed hold such a predicative concept of God; but in Israel the unique achievements of God functioned as proofs of divinity—and obviously the other Gods could never meet them. Such achievements included creating a just society, helping the lowly and the oppressed, explaining the past, and determining the future (e.g. Deutero-Isaiah and Ps. 82).

3. H. H. Rowley, *The Faith of Israel* (London: SCM Press, 1961), 40 ff.

4. C. J. Labuschagne, *The Incomparability of Yahweh in the Old Testament* (Leiden: E. J. Brill, 1966), 92. Most of this last page of the text is taken from *Here Am I,* 140–41.

5. C. Westermann, *Isaiah 40–66* (London: SCM Press, 1969), 15 ff. See also G. von Rad, *Gottes Wirken in Israel* (Neukirchen: Neukirchener Verlag, 1974), 154, 218 ff.

6. Hendrikus Berkhof, *Christian Faith* (Grand Rapids, Mich.: Eerdmans, 1979). See especially chap. 21.

7. Ibid., 510–11.

8. Luke in particular stresses the astonishment of the spectators, as in Luke 2:18, 33, 47; 4:22, 32, 36; 5:9, 26; 7:16–17; 8:25, 56; 9:43; 11:14; 20:26; 24:12, 41. Clearly this is one of Luke's focal and consistent themes—also in Acts, when he describes the people's reaction to the authoritative and convincing actions of the apostles. Here, too, miracles play an important part.

9. This is a dominant theme in John's Gospel especially.

3

A Whiteheadian Theodicy
BOWMAN L. CLARKE

I am personally convinced that the problem of defending God's power and moral goodness in the face of the obvious fact of the existence of evil in the world cannot be treated adequately apart from some philosophical system or framework. By a philosophical system or framework, I mean a consistent and coherent set of very general ideas which we can use to interpret all the elements of our experience, and to tie together our most likely scientific hypotheses, our best ethical insights and our deepest religious experiences into one systematic view of the world. The purpose of this paper is to explore how the problem of evil in relation to God's power and moral goodness would be treated in Whitehead's philosophical framework; in short, to propose a Whiteheadian theodicy. Although Whitehead has a theology and he does make frequent comments on evil, albeit somewhat isolated ones, he never wrote a theodicy as such. The present task is to use Whitehead's philosophical framework for this purpose. In so doing, however, I shall not be interested in defending Whitehead's philosophical framework itself; that is an entirely different problem. First, I shall characterize what I mean by 'an evil' and then I shall propose a classification of evils and consider each class in relation to God's power and moral goodness.

What shall we mean by 'an evil'? It is quite frequent in theodicies to justify some evils on the basis that they are instrumental for some greater good and thus not really evils. To avoid this potential confusion, let us speak in terms of *prima facie* evils, as some ethicists speak of *prima facie* moral obligations. Henceforth, the term 'evil' will be used in this context in the sense of a *prima facie* evil. Let us call any element which is less than desirable in an experience of any kind a *prima facie* evil.

Now let us examine this definition. First, why limit evils to elements in an experience of some kind? I think William James is right; "it appears that such words (such as 'good,' 'evil,' and 'obligation') can have no application or relevancy in a world in which no sentient life exists."[1] Imagine, James goes on to tell us, (if one can), a world in which there is no sentient creature at all, not even a God or an interested observer of any kind—could anything really be called evil in such a world? I personally doubt it. Second, why the phrase "less than desirable"? As Socrates put it, all men desire good. Something good in experience is something desirable, something of value. Evil then is disvalue—something less than the most desirable. For an evil to be present in an experience simply means that what is there is something less than the most desirable.

It has been customary to classify evils into two groups: moral evils and natural evils. Moral evils involved the free moral decisions of creatures, such as the decision to steal or to commit murder. Natural evils were evils due to the forces of nature, such as the suffering and loss due to tornadoes and disease, as well as the suffering due to animals killing and devouring each other, or what Tennyson called "Nature, red in tooth and claw."[2] I would like, however, to revive an older classification of evils into three groups. My classification corresponds to a classification of evils proposed by an Anglican archbishop of the eighteenth century, William King,[3] and was virtually reiterated by Leibniz.[4] I shall call them: (1) evils due to the finitude of creatures; (2) evils due to the free moral decisions of creatures—that is, decisions involving some knowledge of the possible consequences of the decision and some deliberation; and (3) evils due to the environment of creatures, but not involving the free moral decisions of any particular creature. This classification, as we shall see, bears a resemblance to the even more ancient theological triad of evils, death, sin and the devil—provided, of course, the devil is associated with natural evils, which he was.

First, let us look at what I have called evils due to the finitude of creatures. To be a finite creature is to be limited, particularly by the conditions of space and time. Daily, we are forced to choose between two alternatives, both equally desirable, simply because we cannot be in two different places at the same time. We have to choose between being in one environment and being elsewhere experiencing any one of other perhaps equally desirable environments. Most frequently our choices must be between equally desirable alternatives because we are spatially limited to one place. As Whitehead puts it, "The nature of evil is that the characters of things are mutually obstructive. Thus, the depths of life require a process of selection. But selection is elimination."[5] These unactualized desirable alternatives remain forever unexperienced. This is a fact of life.

The finite conditions of time are perhaps far more dramatic, if not more tragic. Given any desirable experience, it is temporary; it will pass. Even the most desirable experience passes. Perhaps one tries to recapture it and hold on to it in memory; but memory fades and finally vanishes. Eventually all our experiences will cease in time and recede farther and farther into the fading past. A visit to the cemetery is a sad substitute for the experience of being with a living loved one. In fact, Whitehead at one point went so far as to say that "the ultimate evil in the temporal world . . . is the fact that the past fades, that time is a perpetual perishing."[6] If evil is something in experience less than desirable, then much evil in experience is due to the finitude of creatures.

The evils due to the finitude of creatures are frequently ignored in the discussions of the problem of evil, probably because we simply accept them as an inevitable part of life. Such things as murder and tornadoes are less frequent and more dramatic, so that moral and natural evils get all the attention. Nevertheless, these evils due to the finitude of creatures have as much right to be called evils as the latter, and need to be considered. How then can we reconcile these evils with the goodness and power of God? The answer here is somewhat obvious: they are inevitable if there are to be finite creatures. God is responsible for these evils insofar as God created the finite creatures. Even God's power, however, cannot create finite creatures which are not finite. The only choice open even to an all-powerful creator is to create finite creatures with the consequent evils of finitude or not to create finite creatures at all. And if the possible good to be actualized in creating finite creatures outweighs the inevitable evils of finitude, then God's creating finite creatures is no threat to the divine moral goodness or power.

The second group of evils I have called "evils due to the free moral decisions of finite creatures." This group of evils, which Archbishop King called "vicious elections," corresponds closely to what has been called moral evils, except I am including both the evil decisions and their evil consequences in this group. Previously, we spoke of our being frequently forced to choose between equally desirable alternatives; but unfortunately, human beings, knowing full well the consequences of their choices, often choose the less desirable alternatives over the more desirable ones. They choose to steal, commit murder, cause other animals to suffer, etc. In fact, we are all so familiar with this from reading the daily newspaper that we need not tarry listing them. The decisions above, however, are the more dramatic and less frequent free moral decisions of creatures that result in evil; otherwise they would not make the newspaper. A very large number of our decisions, however, fail to conform to the ideal in a particular situation, and, as Whitehead notes, "So far as the conformity is incomplete, there is evil in the world."[7]

God's goodness and power have traditionally been defended in the light of evil in the world due to the free decisions of creatures in the following way: God in his goodness created the creatures and endowed them with moral freedom, but God does not make the free moral decisions of the creatures. Therefore, he does not will, or create, evil in this situation but merely permits evil. It is further argued that this does not threaten either God's power or his goodness. If God did not allow free moral creatures the possibility of choosing evil alternatives, they would not be free moral creatures, and the existence of free moral creatures is a good which outweighs the possible evil which results from their free moral decisions. Free moral creatures are taken to be the apex of God's creation. This line of defense with reference to this group of evils has recently come to be called "the free-will defense."

This free-will defense has, however, just as recently come under serious attack. J. L. Mackie puts the attack upon the free-will defense in this way:

If God has made men so that in their free choices they sometimes prefer what is good and sometimes what is evil, why could he not have made men such that they always freely choose the good? If there is no logical impossibility in a man's choosing the good on one, or on several occasions, there can be no impossibility in his freely choosing the good on every occasion.[8]

In short, Mackie is arguing that since it is logically possible, that is, is not self-contradictory, that all persons actualize the best alternative in any free decision, then God could have created us so that we would actualize the best alternative in any free decision. On the surface, this sounds plausible, but there is a subtle bit of sophistry hidden in the argument. Certainly, the sentence "All human beings actualize the best alternative of 'the good,' in their free decision in each situation" is a false sentence, but it is not a self-contradictory one, or at least it certainly does not appear to me to be. Yet the sentence "God can *create* human beings such that they always actualize the best alternative, or 'the good,' in their free decision in each situation" is, in the context of Whitehead's framework, self-contradictory; and, I think, in any other. But this depends upon the meanings of the terms 'create,' 'free,' and most of all 'decision.'

There is a fundamental principle which Whitehead shares with a number of philosophers and theologians in the Christian tradition and one which we would do well to keep in mind throughout all the discussion that follows. It is the principle that it takes as much power for God to sustain creation through any moment of time as it does for any initial creation. The only difference between now and any first moment of creation would be that the first moment came first. God is in fact creating a new creation every moment in time. Every moment is a new creation *ex nihilo;* it is a new coming into being. In fact it is this that gives us our sense of the passage of time. There is a now, and then it is gone, replaced by a new now; and then it is gone, replaced by a new now; and so on. Time is a perpetual perishing and coming into being. This process of the creation of a now, of this coming into being of a here-now, is central to Whitehead's philosophical framework.

The term 'decision' is also important in Whitehead's writings and is closely tied to his rejection of determinism, the belief that every detail of every event is precisely determined by prior events according to a given set of natural laws. Absolute determinism, for him, is a metaphysical dogma that arose with seventeenth century physics and dominated Western thought for three centuries; yet, as Peirce argued, this dogma is not needed by science, cannot possibly be confirmed by science, and has been rejected by contemporary physics. Whitehead, along with philosophers like James, Peirce, and Hartshorne, analyzes the situation in this way: Given any event, with its settled past and the laws of nature, there are always genuine alternatives open for actualization in that event. All of its details are not determined by its past and the laws of nature. To actualize one of these possible alternatives rather than another is a decision. Given the past of any event, Whitehead writes, ". . . whatever is determinable is determined; but there is always a remainder for decision."[9] He uses the term 'decision' in its root meaning. The root meaning of the infinitive 'to decide' is 'to cut off.' To decide is to cut off one alternative of the possible alternatives forever as unactualized possibilities for that particular event. The event could have been slightly different but was not.

In the present context, I have added the adjective 'moral' to the phrase 'free decision,' because of the fact that the actualization of one out of a number of possible alternatives in an event could be a free decision, but not necessarily a free *moral* decision. We usually take freedom, particularly where morality is concerned, to involve not only a free decision but also deliberation concerning consequences. We have some knowledge of the consequences of the actualization of one alternative rather than another, and these consequences are usually taken to be important ones. And we decide one way or the other on this basis. Thus, I take a free moral decision to be a decision that involves some possible knowledge of the possible consequences of the actualization of the possible alternatives and some possibility of deliberation about the possible alternatives.

Let us return now to Mackie's attack on the free-will defense. I said that I considered the statement, "God creates human beings such that they always actualize the best alternatives in their free decisions in every situation," to be, in the context, self-contradictory. Why I do should be clear by now. The problem is the "can create . . . such that." If God created a creature such that it always actualized the best alternative in every situation, it would not then be a free creature: it would have no genuine alternatives to actualize. In creating the creature, God would have made the decisions for the creature. It itself would have no decisions, much less what I have called free moral ones. Decisions are the creature's own contribution to the creation of the moment. No other creature, nor God himself, can make a free creature's decision on it. Parents know they cannot make the decisions of their children; they can only influence them, or limit the possible alternatives for them. In fact, Whitehead would argue that you cannot even make decisions for your own future self. You can plan now, you can make decisions now which limit the possibilities for the future self, and you can influence your future decisions now, but you cannot make them now. Only your future self can do that by actualizing some possible alternatives at that future time. God can decide what the best alternatives for the creatures are, and he does. God can limit the possible alternatives for the creature, and he does. God can try to persuade creatures to make the best decisions, and he does. But it is logically impossible for God to make a decision for a free creature.

Nelson Pike, in his article, "Over-Power and God's Responsibility for Sin," suggests a different way of formulating this attack upon the free-will defense.[10] He proposes that God could limit the alternatives facing the creature at any given moment to good ones. This would not destroy the creature's freedom—the creature still faces genuine alternatives—yet it would eliminate the creature's actualization of evil. This formulation of the objection to the free-will defense appears to escape my above objection to Mackie's formulation. In this way, Pike thinks that God could "prevent wrong action while, at the same time, allowing creatures free will and thus preserving the precondition of morally right action."[11] It does not destroy the freedom of the creature.

Let us look, however, at this alternative formulation. If Pike's suggested attack is going to work, all the real alternatives facing the creature at any given moment must be of equal value; for to allow the creature to choose between alternatives of unequal value still leaves open the possibility of evil. To choose to actualize an alternative of lesser value in a given situation is to actualize evil. If, however, God did limit the free creatures to alternatives of equal value only, in what sense is the creature morally free? Surely deliberation and knowledge of consequences are irrelevant for his decisions. One alternative is as good as the other. He might as well flip a coin in order to choose between them. Decision here is morally neutral; the creature is neither blameworthy nor praiseworthy, and ethics is a subject with no subject matter. Just as Mackie's attack on the free-will defense destroys the freedom in moral freedom, Pike's suggested attack destroys the moral element in moral freedom. If creatures are created so that they can actualize only the best alternative, of which there can be only one, there can be no freedom. If creatures are created so that they can actualize only alternatives of equal value, there is freedom, but there is no moral freedom.

Is the fact that God cannot create free creatures such that they always actualize the best alternative in any given situation, or the fact that God cannot create moral creatures whose decisions are always morally neutral, a limitation on God's power? No, not if it is contradictory for God to make their free decisions or contradictory to create moral creatures who are not moral. It is no more a limitation on God's power than the facts that God cannot create a round square, or that God cannot create a finite creature that is not finite, are limitations on the divine power. There is no such power. As St. Thomas put it a long time ago:

All confess that God is omnipotent, but it seems difficult to explain in what His omnipotence precisely consists. For there may be a doubt as to the precise meaning of the word "all" when we say that God can do all things. If, however, we consider the matter aright, since power is said in reference to possible things, this phrase, *God can do all things,* is rightly understood to mean that God can do all things that are possible.[12]

In short, a contradictory idea of power is an idea of no possible power. God's only alternatives were to create free moral creatures with their possibilities for evil, or to create no free moral creatures at all. But what of God's goodness? In creating free creatures did God not create the possibilities of their evil? Of course, but analogously to the same problem with reference to the evils of finitude, the question boils down to this: Do the opportunities for good in the creation of free moral creatures outweigh the risks of the evil in their creation? If they do, then the evils due to the free moral decisions of creatures are no threat to the moral goodness of God.

There is a third line of argument which I think escapes my above criticisms of Mackie and Pike.[13] One might argue that God could have created human beings morally free and yet created them so that they could not commit the grosser evils. In this way, unlike Mackie's human being, this human being would be free; he could still make genuine free decisions. Also, unlike Pike's human being, this human being could still make free moral decisions between good and evil. The only limitation would be that certain of the grosser evils would be eliminated as genuine possibilities for actualization. As an example, this human being may be free to choose to steal or to lie, but not to commit murder. The elimination of the possibility of some kind of evil usually carries with it a price, and that price is the elimination of some kind of good. Take for example what many would consider the possibility of the greatest evil facing mankind today—the nuclear destruction of the entire human race. Could God eliminate this possibility in creation without severely limiting mankind's knowledge? If it is the case, and it does seem to be the case, that the elimination of the possibility of a particular kind of evil carries with it the elimination of the possibility of some kind of good, then the question for a theodicy here is simply the basic question mentioned above. Do the opportunities for good in the creation of the free moral creatures which God did create outweigh the risks for evil in their creation?

Let us turn now to our third class of evils—evils due to the environment of creatures, but not due to free moral decisions of any creatures. Here we encounter our greatest difficulties, largely due to our own ignorance. As we mentioned earlier, Whitehead rejects absolute determinism, which means that for him every event has open genuine possible alternatives in which certain possibilities are cut off and actualized by free decision. This also means that this situation extends all the way down the scale of nature to the lowliest physical particle. Apart from the free moral decisions of human beings, we know little or nothing of the free decisions of other creatures; that is, what their possible alternatives are. I am sure that it would be safe to say, however, that they are not free moral decisions in the way in which I used the term earlier; that is, the decisions do not involve some knowledge of the consequences and some element of deliberation. No virus scratches his head, contemplates the consequences of possible alternatives and decides to actualize the alternative of attacking me rather than you because of the imagined consequences. However, from the principle of indeterminacy, it does appear that electrons can slightly alter their direction or their velocity. Or, at least, in terms of past events and the laws of nature, we cannot predict precisely where they will be since we cannot determine both their direction and their velocity. This is enough to introduce freedom as we have characterized it, or chance, into nature. Enough so that Einstein wanted to reject the principle because, as he put it, he did not believe that God threw dice. He thought that chance in nature meant that God had created a messy universe.

If we allow free decisions, or chance, in nature, then the only possible answer that could be given to the question, "Why did this particular thing happen to me at that time?" is "It was sheer chance." In other words, it was the result of many free decisions of many creatures, none of which knew of the consequences. In every case, the twisting thread of the course of events in nature is an extremely complicated one, and what free decisions enter into it we can never know. If there are sub-moral free decisions, or chance, in nature, however, then much of the evil due to the particular environment of creatures is due to chance. We must raise the question as to whether free decisions, or chance, limit God's power. And does chance, as Einstein suggests, exist in order to allow God simply to throw dice and create a messy world? Has God not the power to create a neat universe? If there are to be free moral creatures, then I think the answer to these questions is: No. If God did not allow something like free decisions, or chance, on the part of sub-moral creatures, then human beings could not make free moral decisions. The possibility of free moral decisions rests upon there being what I have called free decisions, or chance. In arguing this point, Whitehead in *Science and the Modern World* assumes the thesis, "each molecule blindly runs," and shows what follows from it. And by that thesis he means that every molecular event is absolutely determined by prior events and the mechanical laws of nature; there are no genuine possible alternatives open for it at any point. He argues:

The human body is a collection of molecules. Therefore, the human body blindly runs, and therefore there can be no individual responsibility for the actions of the body. If you once accept that the molecule is definitely determined to be what it is, independently of any determination by reason of the total organism of the body, and if you further admit that the blind run is settled by the general mechanical laws, there can be no escape from this conclusion. [i.e., There is no human responsibility and free moral decision.][14]

In short, absolute determinism abolishes free decisions. We cannot make free moral decisions if every detail of every physical event in our body is already fully determined to be what it is. We cannot even make free decisions.

The difficulty of reconciling absolute determinism with human freedom is dramatically illustrated in Bertrand Russell's "A Free Man's Worship." Russell accepted absolute determinism under the guise of "the world which science presents for our belief":

That man is the product of causes which had no prevision of the end that they were achieving; that his origin, his growth, his hopes and fears, his loves and his beliefs, are but the outcome of accidental collocations of atoms. . . .[15]

Russell accepts this and tells us that "all these things, if not quite beyond dispute are so nearly certain, that no philosophy which rejects them can hope to stand."[16] Then in the next paragraph Russell writes:

Man is yet free, during his brief years, to examine, to criticize, to know, and in imagination to create. To him alone, in the world with which he is acquainted, this freedom belongs; and in this lies his superiority to the resistless forces that control his outward life.[17]

Russell would obviously take the beliefs expressed in "A Free Man's

Worship" to be the result of his own "free examining, criticizing, knowing and imagining." Yet the very printed words which we read in Russell's book, he has told us, are "but the outcome of accidental collocations of atoms," as well as were the vibrations of Russell's vocal cords in dictating them or the movements of his hand in writing them. How is Russell free to create if the movements of his body are "but the outcome of accidental collocations of atoms"? Of course, Russell made it even more paradoxical than this: "his hope, fears, his loves and his beliefs [including Russell's beliefs expressed in "A Free Man's Worship"] are but the outcome of accidental collocations of atoms." Wherein lies Russell's "freedom to criticize, to examine, to know and to create" that constitutes "his superiority to the resistless forces that control his outward life"? Modern philosophy is filled with paradoxical, if not contradictory, statements such as Russell's, albeit not always so dramatic. The history of the universe, according to Whitehead, is a story in the process of being written, and it is the outcome of numberless free decisions, both moral and non-moral, among which are the decisions of God. And this is the way it must be, if there are to be free moral decisions. There is no other alternative for God in creating free moral creatures.

The chance decisions of creatures, however, cannot fully account for all the evils in this third group. Some of the evils in this class are simply due to there being a multitude of different kinds of creatures and their being the kinds they are. That that particular cat ate that particular rat at that particular time might be a matter of chance, but cats by nature seem to eat rats when they get a chance. This may be in the best interest of cats and ourselves, but it is not in the best interest of the rats. Some types of viruses need human cells as host, if they are going to survive and reproduce. To attack human beings is in the best interest of the viruses, but not in the best interest of human beings. The lion and lamb may lie down together, but it is not likely in this world, in which it is rather risky for the lamb. Tennyson is right: nature is "red in tooth and claw"—and we are a part of it. We enjoy our steak at the expense of the best interest of the cow. Every kind of creature from the highest to the lowliest physical particle needs energy to survive and perpetuate itself in time, and that energy often comes at the expense of other creatures. With a multiplicity of kinds of creatures, there inevitably comes a multiplicity of kinds of interest and, consequently, conflicts of interest. On one hand, we are all robbers. The kinds of creatures in nature form an intricate web of conflict of interest; but also of mutual help and dependence; of mutual destruction, but also of cooperation of interest; of evil, but also of good. Whitehead notes this fact of dependence, help, and cooperation of the various kinds, or species, of creatures in *Science and the Modern World*. He writes:

> . . . there are associations of different species which mutually cooperate. This differentiation of species is exhibited in the simplest physical entities, such as the association between electrons and positive nuclei, and in the whole realm of animate nature. The trees in a Brazilian forest depend upon the association of various species of organisms, each of which is mutually dependent on the other species. . . . A forest is the triumph of the organization of mutual dependent species.[18]

Ecologists are just beginning to help us to see how intrinsic this web of dependence and cooperation in nature really is.

What now can be said in defense of the power and goodness of God in light of this vast multitude of different kinds of creatures woven into a vast web of mutual conflict and mutual cooperation? Certainly there is no problem with the power of God as such. In fact, the variety and multitude of creatures have always been taken to be a testimony to God's power. It is the moral goodness of God which is called into question when one focuses on the instances of conflict of interest, rather than cooperation, in this intricate web of nature. What could be the good of the whole which could justify the evil produced by this conflict of interest? Any of us who had a chance of planning this intricate web of nature would certainly leave out of it those creatures whose interests tend to conflict with our own. If the rats had the opportunity to design it, they would clearly leave out the cats, to say nothing of leaving out human beings with their Orkin men. And the lambs, no doubt, would exclude the lions. I began by identifying the good with the desirable, but desirable to whom?—in this case, to which kinds of creatures? Multiplicity of different kinds of creatures inevitably leads to a conflict as to which kinds of creatures are desirable. Which kind of creature you find desirable depends upon which kind of creature you are. What is the good or the desirable in this case?

Whitehead maintains that "all order is aesthetic order; and the moral order is merely certain aspects of aesthetic order."[19] A moral decision, action, habit, or rule is morally good because it contributes to the aesthetic good. Thus, in *Adventures of Ideas* he says, "The real world is good when it is beautiful."[20] He is using the term 'beautiful' in the ancient Greek and Medieval sense of 'harmonious.' In harmony, according to him, "the parts contribute to the massive feeling of the whole, and the whole contributes to the intensity of feeling of the parts."[21] Harmony, therefore, is based on variety in unity. It is exemplified in what we have been describing as the intricate web of nature. To emphasize variety at the expense of unity is to lead to discord, conflict, and mutual destruction. To emphasize unity at the expense of variety is to lead to mere repetition, triviality, and boredom. The trick of harmony is to strike a happy medium between variety and unity. God has apparently designed the multiplicity of creatures in this world with enough variety to keep it interesting, exciting and alive, and with enough unity to keep the conflict of interest from destroying it. As such, Whitehead would say, it exemplifies harmony and is good, and God's decision to create it, consequently, is morally good.

The universe, as we have pictured it, is a vast society of a multitude of different kinds of creatures interwoven with conflicts of interest and interdependence. The particular history of this universe is the story which is the outcome of all their free decisions, both free non-moral decisions and free moral decisions, within the limits of the natural laws of the kinds of creatures which are due to the decisions of God. It is a very risky environment, indeed, in which to live, due to the multitude of kinds of creatures and their free decisions. But it is a universe filled with possibilities for good, as well as risks of evil. And the risks of evil cannot be avoided if the possibilities for good are to be there. Charles Hartshorne has put it this way:

God adjusts basic kinds of possibility of good and evil as inherent in certain laws of nature. The rest is simply what the creatures happen to decide. Those who ask for a world without freedom and risk are also asking for one without opportunity. Indeed they know not what they ask. . . . Without the risks there could not be the opportunities, and the opportunities are divinely judged as worth the risks.[22]

This question of whether or not the opportunities for good are worth the risks in the possibilities of evil has been dramatically posed by Dostoyevsky in *The Brothers Karamazov*. He puts the problem in terms of whether all the good in creation is worth the suffering of one tiny child, and he has Ivan ask Alyosha,

"Tell me yourself, I challenge you—answer. Imagine that you are creating a fabric of human destiny . . . , but that it was essential and inevitable to torture to death only one tiny creature—that baby . . . , for instance—and to found that edifice on its unavenged tears, would you be the architect on those conditions? Tell me and tell me the truth." "No, I wouldn't consent," said Alyosha softly.[23]

There is only one catch to this dramatic way of putting the problem. As I suggested earlier, we are co-creators of this world each moment of our lives. Suicide is a genuine alternative. But we not only continue to create this world every moment by our free decisions, we also continue to bring children into this world. If we were honest, I think we would have to admit that we do in fact believe that the possibilities for good in the universe do outweigh all the risks of evil.

If God is morally good and has created a world in which the possibility of evil exists, then God cannot be indifferent to that evil; God must seek to overcome it. In Whitehead's philosophical scheme, God is everlastingly luring the creatures to actualize the better alternatives at any one moment. God is himself everlastingly seeking to overcome evil in the world. However, as Madden and Hare have pointed out, as long as the creatures have the power of free decision, there is no assurance that good will triumph in time.[24] Creatures everlastingly have the power of resisting God. Also, as we suggested earlier, the evils due to the finitude of creatures can never be overcome in the world; space *is* limiting, and time *is* a perpetual perishing.

God, however, does not remain indifferent to evil for Whitehead, even when God is rejected. In the divine experience, God knows immediately all the value and joy as well as the suffering in the experiences of the creatures. In taking up the joys of the creatures, God preserves them everlastingly in the divine experience. Thus, the perpetual perishing of time is overcome in God. Nothing good in any creaturely experience is ever lost. In taking up the sufferings of the creatures into the divine experience, God suffers with them, and in so doing, to use Whitehead's phrase, "God is the great companion—the fellow sufferer who understands."[25] God, however, does not merely suffer with the creatures; in taking suffering up into the divine experience, God overcomes it. By taking up the evils of the world into the divine experience, evil is overcome. Even though good may not triumph in time, it does in God. Perhaps it is better to let Whitehead speak for himself here. This triumph is, according to him, "the story of the dynamic effort of the World passing into everlasting unity, and of the static majesty of God's vision, accomplishing its purpose of completion by absorption of the World's multiplicity of effort."[26] And he goes on to add: "It is in this way that the immediacy of sorrow and pain is transformed into an element of triumph. This is the notion of redemption through suffering which haunts the world."[27]

NOTES

1. William James, "The Moral Life and the Moral Philosopher," in *Essays in Pragmatism*, ed. Alburey Castell (New York: Hafner, 1969), 69.

2. Alfred Lord Tennyson, "In Memoriam," *Alfred Tennyson: "In Memoriam", "Maud," & Other Poems*, ed. John D. Jump (Totowa, N.J.: Rowman, 1974), section 56, line 4.

3. William King, *An Essay on the Origin of Evil*, 4th ed., trans. Edmund Law (Cambridge: Cambridge University Press, 1958) 92.

4. Gottfried W. Leibniz, *Theodicy*, trans. E. M. Huggard (London: Routledge and Kegan Paul, 1952), par. 21.

5. Alfred N. Whitehead, *Process and Reality* (New York: Macmillan, 1929), 517.

6. Ibid., 517.

7. Whitehead, *Religion in the Making* (New York: Meridian Books, 1960), 60.

8. J. L. Mackie, "Evil and Omnipotence," in *Good and Evil*, ed. Nelson C. Pike (Englewood Cliffs, N.J.: Prentice-Hall, 1964), 56.

9. Whitehead, *Process and Reality*, 41.

10. Nelson C. Pike, "Over-Power and God's Responsibility for Sin," in *God and Temporality*, ed. Bowman L. Clarke and Eugene T. Long (New York: Paragon House, New ERA Books, 1984).

11. Ibid.

12. St. Thomas Aquinas, *Summa Theologica*, 1, q. 25, a. 3. Tha above quote is from the Anton C. Pegis revision of the English Dominican translation in *Basic Writings of Saint Thomas Aquinas* (New York: Random House, 1945).

13. This was suggested to me in conversation by John K. Roth. See also Roth's critique of David R. Griffin's Whiteheadian theodicy in *Encountering Evil: Live Options in Theodicy*, ed. Stephen T. Davis (Atlanta: John Knox Press, 1981), 119–22.

14. Alfred N. Whitehead, *Science and the Modern World* (New York: The New American Library, 1956), 79.

15. Bertrand Russell, "A Free Man's Worship," in *Mysticism and Logic* (Garden City, N.Y.: Doubleday, 1957), 45.

16. Ibid.

17. Ibid., 46.

18. Whitehead, *Science and the Modern World*, 206.

19. Whitehead, *Religion in the Making*, 101.

20. Alfred N. Whitehead, *Adventures of Ideas* (New York: Macmillan, 1933), 345.

21. Ibid., 324.

22. Charles Hartshorne, "A New Look at the Problem of Evil," in *Current Philosophical Issues: Essays in Honor of Curt John Ducasse,* ed. F. C. Dommeyer (Springfield, Ill.: Charles C. Thomas, 1966), 208.

23. Fyodor Dostoyevsky, *The Brothers Karamazov,* trans. Constance Garnett (New York: Random House, 1950), 291.

24. Edward H. Madden and Peter H. Hare, *Evil and the Concept of God* (Springfield, Ill.: Charles C. Thomas, 1966), 208.

25. Whitehead, *Process and Reality*, 532.

26. Ibid., 530.

27. Ibid., 531.

4

Is God Good and Can God Be Defended?

LLOYD EBY

I have perceived the question of the defense of God in legal fashion—as both a series of indictments and a defense against these indictments—and have structured this paper accordingly. The first section lists some important indictments against God. The next attempts to say something about the distinction between God and religion. This distinction is important because most of the indictments are really against religion more than God. The third part is sectarian; since I am a member of the Unification Church, I feel I should present a Unification theodicy based on Unification theology, the best theology I know, and one that has important similarities with process thought. The fourth and final section of the paper presents an account of the theodicy of Dostoevsky's *The Brothers Karamazov,* along with some comments from Albert Camus's commentary on it. Dostoevsky gives one of the best literary presentations of the problem of theodicy—along with a solution—that I know about, and in addition, he speaks to certain existential issues that most other accounts ignore.

Most people who are concerned with theology or the philosophy of religion seem to think that the existence of God is the most important problem, but for a long time I have felt that a far more important question is whether God—who I am sure enough exists—is good. The question of the goodness of God has two parts: (1) can God do away with the evils that befall humankind, (i.e., the problem of theodicy), and (2) does God really sufficiently desire human happiness and well-being? In my view, a defense of God requires that these two questions be answered in such a way that we can be convinced that God is indeed good (i.e., sufficiently concerned with human happiness and well-being) and that God is sufficiently concerned with doing away with evil.

I myself have a fear that God may not be good. This fear no doubt has something to do with my having grown up within an overwhelming and oppressive religious tradition. Sometimes, in fact, I have the attitude that I would like to be able to bring God up on charges of criminal negligence, an attitude which is, of course, impious and destructive. This question of God's goodness is, therefore, of more than academic interest to me, and I suspect that my attitude on this is not unique but is characteristic of at least a significant number of people today. It is also an old question, at least as old at Plato's *Euthyphro,* in which Socrates asks whether the good is good because the gods love it, or whether the gods love what is good because it is good. Many pious people *do* understand goodness in terms of union with God or conformity with divine will, but many other people question whether God is really good. Therefore, whatever the sensibilities of religious people, it is necessary that the question of God's goodness be explored.

Indictments Against God or Religion

Many indictments have been issued against God and religion. It seems to me that these indictments all have certain features in common. All of them charge God or religion with compromising or diminishing human happiness or well-being in some way, and they all assume (usually tacitly) that goodness is to be understood or defined in terms of promoting human happiness or well-being. In effect, then, the indictments charge God or religion with failing in some important way to be good. As we will see, these indictments come from both the arts and the (putative) sciences.

The Charge of Religious Oppression. As a young person, I felt smothered and overwhelmed by the traditions, requirements, and prohibitions of the religion in which I grew up, which was Mennonitism. At the same time, however, I felt that it truly embodied the will of God, and that God had ultimate claim on me and on the world. Therefore either to accept the religious tradition or to go against it meant that I was doomed; accepting the religious tradition meant unhappiness, but rejecting it meant damnation. There seemed no way out of the dilemma, and that trauma has affected me to this day.

My own experience is personal and unique, but there are enough descriptions of similar binds, given in literature and drama, to suggest that this may be the common lot of many people, especially young people. Examples exist for many different religions. For Roman Catholicism there is the current drama by Christopher

Durang, *Sister Mary Ignatius Explains It All For You,* and James Joyce's novel, *A Portrait of the Artist as a Young Man.* For Judaism there is Chaim Potok's *My Name Is Asher Lev,* in which a young man goes through a great deal of tension because he wants to be an artist, but his orthodox tradition does not welcome the making of images. There are hints in current news stories that many people in certain Islamic situations, such as current day Iran, may be undergoing similar tensions.

This indictment may be summed up as charging that religion or religious traditions are repressive, producing tension and unhappiness, and furthermore that they render it impossible to escape the difficulty because they make people believe that the repression is necessary.

An Indictment from the Arts. In the preceeding subsection, two novels and a drama were mentioned as containing indictments of religion. I believe that these literary works exhibit a general problem of Western arts of the twentieth century. Those arts with the greatest aesthetic and intellectual "bite" are—with some notable exceptions—generally nonreligious and quite often explicitly antireligious. Examples could no doubt be given from all the arts, but I am most familiar with film, and there the evidence seems overwhelming. Antireligious themes occur or predominate in the films of Eisenstein, Buñuel, Cocteau, Hawks, Bergman, Fellini, Coppola, Altman, Fassbinder, and many others. In fact, one is hard-pressed to think of many recent examples of films or dramas in which religion is seen as a force for goodness, creativity, and well-being, especially among the films or dramas that play in the "important" theatres or in the major cities. Films or dramas in which religion is presented in a positive light are generally found in explicitly religious contexts or outlets (churches, religious media or publications, and so on). I do not know the reason for this situation in the arts, and I admit that there are important counterexamples (e.g., *Rocky II, Star Wars,* some films of Capra, Bresson, and Dreyer), but I think that my claim is essentially accurate. There seems to be an assumption today in much of the arts that the religious view is artistically, intellectually, and even socially defective, and that it is subversive of artistic and human well-being.

The Indictment from the Existence of Evil. The classic problem of evil is well-known to all philosophers and theologians: if God is both good and powerful, then why doesn't God use this power to curb evil. God seems to allow (or even encourage!) war, the killing of innocent children, the starvation of masses, and so on. Most devout theodicies have adopted some form of the free will defense. It assumes that evil comes about because humans were given free will by God but they use that free will in such a way as to bring about evil. The value of human free will is taken to be greater than the value that would be achieved if human free will were abrogated by divine intervention. The existence of evil as an indictment of God remains as one of the most difficult problems, however, especially in light of such monstrous twentieth century evils as Fascism, the Holocaust, and the murders of many millions of innocent people at the hands of Communists, as has occurred in the Soviet Union, China, Korea, Cambodia and elsewhere.

The Darwinist Indictment. Whatever Darwin's personal view of religion may have been, his work had the effect of charging religion with being both factually false and intellectually misleading on the question of the origin of species. According to Darwinism, natural selection—and not God—causes change from one biological species to another, and attention to religion causes one to look in the wrong place for an explanation of change of species. *The Origin of Species* does away with divine causation by introducing the materialistic principle of natural selection. However much they may disagree with Darwin on other points today, most biologists hold to these views about religion and would agree with T. H. Huxley, who claimed, "The publication of *The Origin of Species* marks the Hegira of Science from the idolatries of special creation to the purer faith of Evolution."[1]

The Marxist Indictment. We might summarize Marx's well-known criticisms of religion by saying that he held that religion is both factually false (because it is material factors and not spiritual ones that are ultimately responsible for both the superstructure of existence and for the movements of history) and morally and ethically reprehensible (because religion is an opiate which dulls the consciousness of the masses of workers and makes them accept their own exploitation instead of rising up to throw off their chains).

The Freudian Indictment. Freud saw religion as conflicting with sexuality and held that sexality must supersede religion. Freud made much of his own irreligiousness, replacing the image and power of religion and God with another compelling and powerful factor, the factor of sexuality. Jung reports:

I can still recall vividly how Freud said to me, "My dear Jung, promise me never to abandon the sexual theory. That is the most essential thing of all. You see, we must make a dogma of it, an unshakable bulwark." . . . In some astonishment I asked him, "A bulwark—against what?" To which he replied "Against the black tide of mud"—and here he hesitated for a moment, then added—"of occultism."

. . . What Freud seemed to mean by "occultism" was virtually everything that philosophy and religion . . . had learned about the psyche.[2]

To be sure, Jung disagreed with Freud on this. But even today many people interpret Freudianism and other psychological theories as having shown that religion must be opposed because it interferes with healthy or normal sexuality.

An Indictment from Philosophy. A prominent philosopher recently declared to me that anyone who believes in God will come to some point in his intellectual efforts where he abandons philosophy or thought in favor of his dogma or belief. In this view, belief ultimately creates intellectual dishonesty or at least an abandonment of intellect. This view might also be put this way: religious belief, or belief in God, is intellectually demeaning, and hence demeaning of human well-being because human well-being is bound up with intellectual thoroughness, and religious belief prevents intellectual thoroughness.

The Charge That Religion Fosters Conflict and War. Many examples can be given of political conflicts and wars that arise out of religious differences. These facts have often been cited as showing that it is religion itself that makes people hate and oppose one another. It has been assumed that people would be naturally peaceful and harmonious, were it not for religion. In this view religion is the principal cause of disharmony, and harmony would erupt if religion were done away with.

I cannot answer all these indictments here; many of them have been handled more than adequately elsewhere. But all of them have some plausibility, and each seems to rest on at least partial truth. So an adequate defense of God and religion must deal with them somewhere.

God and Religion

Most of the indictments given above are against religion or particular religions. Even if those indictments are accurate, this does not necessarily mean that God is subject to criticism. It is entirely possible that any religion, or even that all religions, misrepresent God.

The claim made by religions that they base their beliefs or practices on revelation does not show that those beliefs or practices really represent the divine will. Every instance of revelation, without exception, requires human reception before it can be represented in belief or practice. So every revelation relies on human intervention, and no one can ever correctly say that any belief or practice is of God without possibility of human error. Religions and religious persons must therefore always remain modest and diffident about their supposed apprehension of divine intention or will.

The fact that religions do disagree shows that at best one of them can be completely correct. More likely, none is.

The fact that every major religion has had some opening to novelty—typically through a mystical tradition—shows that they have recognized that they did not have final or complete truth.

If God is infinite—as most of the major religions have held—then God cannot be comprehended in any one finite text, tradition, or individual human person. Any religion that claims such a complete comprehension for its texts, traditions, or persons is therefore mistaken, as a fact of logic.

One way we can explain the task or purpose of religion is that it is to mediate between God and humans. If they really wish to hold that God is good (as they all have), then religions have the task of showing this; and if anyone thinks or fears that God is not good, then some or all religions have failed in their central purpose. Accusations against God are therefore actually indictments of religion. Religions and religious people have responsibility to speak for God, and religious dissension and chaos are some of the strongest clues that religions are unfaithful to their task.

Since there is a universal human tendency to praise tolerance, civility, unity, helpfulness and humility, and to condemn divisiveness and intolerance, anyone who urges a partisan view in the name of religion, of God, or of revelation, has the duty of showing the efficacy of this particular view for universal human well-being. Claims that "what now appears evil will be good in the long run" must be justified by appealing to observable or public human experience, and not to something that can be shown only through faith or through reference to future time or future experience. Without this public evidence, there is no way of deciding between competing faith-assertions except on the basis of a further faith-assertion.

Unification Theodicy

Rather than go over received theodicies, I will go directly to an account of Unification theodicy. Since Unification texts or official writings do not contain an explicit theodicy, but do say things from which a theodicy can be extracted, this will be an effort at constructive theologizing, based on Unification texts and Unification doctrine.[3]

The Unification Account of Creation. Unification doctrine holds that there were indeed an original and unique man and woman—the biblical Adam and Eve—who were historical persons, created by God and in the image of God. This pair was created to be the primordial parents of the human race.[4]

God's most fundamental aspect is "heart" or purposeful love, and in addition God has dual characteristics or essentialities of both internal character and external form; these dual essentialities occur in everything God creates. In human beings, they are "mind" and "body." God is also of a being of both masculinity and femininity, and (only) man and woman *together* fully represent the image of God.

There is a distinction between spirit and mind, and also between spiritual reality and physical reality. During their physical lifetimes, human beings have both spiritual existence (spiritual mind and spiritual body) and physical existence (physical mind and physical body). Their spiritual existence remains eternally (in the future) but their physical existence was created to be temporal, and physical death was part of the original creation. The spiritual body exists in the realm of spiritual existence; this realm is called the "invisible substantial world," and it is also the realm of existence of angels, who have spiritual minds and bodies but not physical ones. In the spiritual realm direct communication with God is possible. The physical realm (called the "visible substantial world") is the world of physical activity, in which plants and animals and humans (during their physical lives) live. Physical life is also the primary domain for spiritual development because spiritual development requires both "life elements" from God as well as "vitality elements" from the physical realm. Humans are unique in that they exist in both worlds, linking the two together.

The process of development is very important to the Unification view. The original man and woman were put into the garden (the physical world). Told by God that they were to have dominion over it (loving control and stewardship), they could eat of any tree, save the tree of knowledge of good and evil. This commandment is interpreted to mean that they were not to have a sexual relationship until they were sufficiently developed—sufficiently mature—so that the divine prohibition could be removed. Until then they were not in the realm of God's "direct dominion," but once they entered this realm then no sin or deviation from God would be possible and they would be free to have a divinely sanctioned marriage. It was necessary that they first be in the immature state and that they pass through it while keeping the commandment so that they would develop the ability to rule themselves and so that they would have the proper authority and ability to rule over all of creation as God's agents. Thus, they would "inherit God's creativity." When they completed this process, they would attain deity and perfection. In that state no fall would be possible, and they would have a perfect relationship with God. When they died physically, they would pass into the spiritual world and there continue in this relationship with God and with their fellows (husband and wife, parent and child, friend and friend, and so on) eternally. In the Unification view, perfection is a *relation* between the individual and God and between people and other people.

The Unification Account of the Fall. The imperfect man and woman were prohibited from having a sexual relation because God foresaw that in their immaturity they would be susceptible to this temptation. Also, sexual relations have ontological consequences; if this relation were entered into immaturely, this love would separate the participant from the love relation with God. After maturity the sexual relation would only deepen or multiply the divine love. God created this force of love to be the strongest in the universe so that the relation between God and human, between parent and child, and between spouses could be based on something other than law. With love as the strongest force, God could then relate to and guide humankind eternally through the force of love. But because love is the strongest force, it is also the most susceptible of misuse, and this is in fact what happened in the fall.

The angels were created *temporally prior* to humans, but *ontologically* and in divine intention they are *secondary* to humans.[5] They were created to be God's messengers and servants, and to assist God in caring for the human race. Angels (God's servants) are supposed to be subservient to humans (God's children).

Since the angels temporally were prior to humans, they enjoyed God's unchallenged love and attention until the appearance of humans. When the original man and woman appeared, these were God's children, and the angels were to give place to them, become God's servants, and minister to them. This, however, did not occur as God hoped; the archangel Lucifer became jealous and envious because he felt that the love God was giving to Adam and Eve eclipsed the love given to him. Actually, the love Lucifer now received was the same as before, but it seemed less to him because it was overshadowed by the love given to the humans. Lucifer was attracted to Eve, the female, because he was a male spirit; and since Lucifer had aided God in creation he was very knowledgable, which made him attractive to Eve. Their growing closeness changed them, and finally Eve succumbed to Lucifer's attractions and submitted to a sexual relation (through their spiritual bodies) with him; this was the spiritual fall. Eve became spiritually dead—fallen and disconnected from God. The archangel lost his position as God's chief servant and became Satan, God's enemy. Eve inherited fear from the archangel; "her eyes were opened" and she realized that Adam, and not the angel, was her intended husband.

After her fall, Eve wished to regain her status with God, and Adam seemed very attractive to her because he still had his relationship with God. Realizing that Adam was her intended husband, she turned to him, hoping that through a sexual union with him she could reunite with God and regain her former status. Because of his immaturity, Adam's latent sexuality was aroused. He became drawn to her, and a sexual union ensued. But this union, too, was without God's sanction and therefore constituted a second fall, the physical fall, in which Adam also lost his union with God. Rather than solving the problem, Eve's union with Adam compounded it. In effect, both Adam and Eve died as children of God and became the children of Satan through these two acts. The human race thus had no one who could serve as its mediator with God. All subsequent people have inherited the fallen condition of the first parents and are under the (partial) dominion of Satan.

The major results of the fall were that God's plan for the human race was thwarted, Satan came into existence as a powerful force who would be the adversary of God and the dominator of the human race, and the human race came to possess and perpetuate a fallen nature. God's plan for the human race can be summarized in the so-called Three Great Blessings: (1) individual perfection or union with God, (2) family perfection, or marriage and family life, and (3) human dominion over the rest of creation, including the angels. The fallen nature can be characterized in four main aspects: failure to take God's viewpoint, leaving the proper position, reversal of dominion, and the multiplication or enhancement of evil. Our fallen nature is expressed in such things as selfishness, irresponsibility, arrogance, and a desire to involve others in evil actions. These traits were exhibited by the archangel in his dealings with Eve and Adam, and they have been passed on to all subsequent humans as an inheritance from their parents. Satan came into a position where he could separate humankind from God's goodness, and he continues to exercise (partial) dominion over the human race and human affairs to this day. Because God's happiness is conditional on his relationship with humans, God is also sad and burdened—even wretched, because of the human fall.

Toward a Unification Theodicy. Unification texts do not explicitly raise the question of God's goodness, but instead assume that God is wholly good and the source of all goodness. The claim that evil may have preceded the fall or may be inherent in creation is denied.

Freedom was not the cause of the fall, although it is true that without freedom the fall could not have occurred. If freedom were the cause, then even perfected people would be in danger of falling, and insecurity would exist eternally. Had Adam and Eve been sufficiently free, they would not have fallen; they were supposed to reach perfection by the exercise of their free will, but lack of freedom brought about by the force of unprincipled love caused their deviation from goodness. As a result, their freedom was curtailed, since they could no longer have free interchange with God, and they became subject instead to the unfree dominion of Satan and evil.

God's comandment was not the cause of the fall or of evil. The possibility of unprincipled love was inherent in the situation, and the commandment was a warning designed to protect them against this eventuality. Humans were created as they were (imperfect and vulnerable to the possibility of evil) so that they could be other than animals or robots.

Human responsibility is essential, and even God cannot escape the consequences of human choice. There is a part of the responsibility for accomplishment of the divine economy that is God's and a part that is humankind's; God cannot interfere with the part that belongs to humans. Therefore, God is not exactly omnipotent or free, in the usual understanding of those concepts, but is constrained by human choice. Once God gave this power to humans it could not be rescinded because to do so would be to introduce either divine inconsistency or accommodation to an evil principle. God's foreknowledge is also limited; God foresees future possibilities, but does not necessarily know what choices the particular people will actually make. God predestines and foreordains certain characters and situations, as well as the consequences of the situations, but the actual detailed outcome depends on human choice.

Unification theology discusses the question of God's power versus the existence of evil in an unusual way. The *Divine Principle* asks why God did not intervene to prevent the fall and gives three answers: (1) God had established the principle which limited his dominion over imperfect people, and to intervene would have meant violating his own principle; (2) Adam and Eve were to reach perfection by the responsible exercise of their free will in order that they would become qualified for dominion over creation; if God had intervened they would have attained this dominion without the proper qualifications; and (3) since a relationship affects both parties, if God had intervened it would have meant his acknowledging Satan as a co-creator. For all these reasons, then, God could not and cannot intervene in evil and dissolve or prevent it by divine fiat.

Sinlessness and perfection are different. Before the fall, Adam and Eve were without sin, although they were imperfect. They had the relationship with God appropriate to their immaturity (called the "indirect dominion of God"), but after the fall they lost this relationship. Imperfection admits the *possibility* of sin, but does not itself lead to or require sin. Perfection (called the "direct dominion of God") is the state in which no sin is possible because the relationship with God is so strong. *Sinless* imperfection is also a state of divine grace and goodness, even though it is a state of vulnerability. But vulnerability itself is not sinful.

In Unification theory the basis of ontology is relationships, so relations are consequential for those who are related. If Adam and Eve relate with God, they will have godly qualities, but if they relate with any being on an ungodly basis, then they will acquire ungodly qualities. In a similar way, Unification theory holds that the characteristics of the higher position are passed on to the lower (as especially in the case of parents to children). The archangel usurped the higher position in his relation with Eve and gave her certain characteristics that were passed on to Adam, then to all their children, and so on to the subsequent human race. Evil, then, is created by these acts and naturally perpetuated, and God must permit it because God must abide by the principle of creation. Evil is not something that God creates or is responsible for, but it is the natural consequence of the fall, a consequence that God warned of in giving the commandment to refrain from "eating the fruit."

Sexuality itself is not evil, but because of the fall all of human sexuality has become tainted. Tainted or problematic sexuality was not part of the divine plan. In effect, because of the fall, Satan came to partially dominate all of human sexuality. This situation is not permanent, but it must be undone. The original state must be *restored.* Freud was mistaken in claiming that religion interferes with healthy sexuality because there is no completely healthy sexuality until the process of restoration is accomplished. Religions may have contributed to confusion and difficulty on the question of sexuality, but they are only responding to the problem, not causing it.

Satan came into a position to exercise control over the human race as a result of the fall, but Satan is not completely powerful and God is not completely powerless. Fallen people are in a "midway position" between God and Satan, and both God and Satan have a claim on every person. In the struggle for dominance between God and Satan, human choice and human action determine the outcome. God did institute the *Providence of Restoration* in order to undo the consequences of the fall, but this providence too requires human choice and action for its realization.[6] Human choice and action are thus central in determining both human fate and the working of divine providence.

Unification theology denies that what are traditionally called natural evils are really evil. In an ideal world, humans would have mastery over nature in such a way as to eliminate or curtail such things as diseases and natural disasters. Moral evils, however, are a genuine and enormous problem, and they must be done away with before goodness can prevail. (Unificationism rejects any *felix culpa* account of evil.) Evil hurts humans enormously; there was no divine intention that those evils occur, and they hurt God even more than humans, if that is possible.

There is no eternal damnation; eventually all must be saved, even Satan, so no situation, however miserable, is eternally hopeless.

This may be scant hope, but it is infinitely greater than the hopelessness of some theodicies, such as Calvinism or Augustinianism. Even God's happiness depends on the happiness of his creatures; God cannot be happy until every person is happy and so God cannot permanently ignore any person's misery.

The Theodicy of Dostoevsky's *The Brothers Karamazov*

The existential problem concerning evil, as I see it, is whether evil and rebellion against God may be preferable to union with God, even if this leads to damnation. A closely related question is whether an art with aesthetic and intellectual "bite" can be constructed today on a God-affirming or religion-affirming basis. I think that Dostoevsky's *The Brothers Karamazov* speaks to both questions better than perhaps any other work I know.[7]

The indictments against God and religion in this novel occur primarily in Ivan's speech during a long conversation with his younger brother, Alyosha. Ivan begins by declaring his love of life, despite whatever might occur and despite logic. He then states that the eternal questions—God and socialism—must be settled. He affirms belief in God and in an underlying order and meaning to life, but he quickly moves from that to a declaration that he cannot accept God's world because that world is unjust.

To support his charge of injustice, Ivan gives many harrowing and heartrending stories of the suffering of innocent children. These stories are so moving that finally Alyosha—a novice—agrees that he too would want the perpetrators of these injustices shot. Ivan then pounces on this admission, and declares that it shows that the world is absurd. He demands retribution, and not in some infinite time or space, but here on earth. He rejects the view that there is some higher harmony that these things serve, declares that he could not accept any harmony that required the intense sufferings of such innocent children, and ends with a statement of rebellion against God, saying: "It's not God that I don't accept, Alyosha, only I most respectfully return Him the ticket."[8]

The force of Ivan's indictment of the world's injustice is so great that he compels even Alyosha to admit that the situation as described requires rebellion.

"Rebellion? I am sorry you call it that," said Ivan earnestly. "One can hardly live in rebellion, and I want to live. Tell me yourself, I challenge you—answer. Imagine that you are creating a fabric of human destiny with the object of making men happy in the end, giving them peace and rest at last, but that it was essential and inevitable to torture to death only one tiny creature—that baby, beating its breast with its fist, for instance—and to found that edifice on its unavenged tears, would you consent to be the architect on those conditions? Tell me, and tell the truth."

"No, I wouldn't consent," said Alyosha softly.[9]

Alyosha tries to protest that Christ—because he gave his innocent blood for all and everything—is the being on whom a foundation for the edifice of justice and forgiveness is constructed. Ivan rejects this possibility, too, in the well-known chapter entitled "The Grand Inquisitor." Although this chapter should be understood in terms of Dostoevsky's Slavophile attack on the Roman Catholic Church, it can also be seen as an attack on organized or institutional Christian religion in general. Religion has rendered ineffective Christ's attempt at liberation, replacing it with central planners who understand that the masses of people are too weak and too desirous of comfort, regularity, and material well-being to be able to follow and benefit from Christ's work and teaching. The Church (churches) has gone over to the devil but for good reasons; that side gives the bread, the peace, and the power over kingdoms of the earth that Jesus rejected. The Grand Inquisitor has gone over to that side not for personal gain, but out of love for humanity because he realized that this way was the only way that could truly offer benefit to the struggling and unruly masses of people.

Albert Camus' comments on this novel are most astute. He notes that Ivan's rebellion goes beyond previous rebels against God, whose rebellion was primarily individualistic. Ivan changes the tone, goes beyond reverential blasphemy, and puts God himself on trial.

If evil is essential to divine creation, then creation is unacceptable. Ivan will no longer have recourse to this mysterious God, but to a higher principle—namely, justice. He launches the essential undertaking of rebellion, which is that of replacing the reign of grace by the reign of justice. He simultaneously begins the attack on Christianity.[10]

Ivan makes these attacks not because he does not believe in God, but because he feels that God is unjust and hence evil. He ranks justice above the divinity, and refutes God in the name of moral value. Ivan attacks the interdependence in Christianity between suffering and truth. His rejection is so total that even if offered salvation or eternal life he would refuse, because to accept it would mean acquiescence to the injustice of the world.

The problem with Ivan's total rejection of divine coherence, however, is that this stance leads to recognizing the legitimacy of murder and to the condoning of crime. Once he has taken this step of rebellion, he must go to its bitter end, which is to replace God with man—a metaphysical revolution in which man occupies the place formerly held by God. [11]

But Ivan's rebellion leads to contradiction; there is now no basis on which to distinguish between what is permissible and what is crime. One man's view of what is permissible becomes as legitimate as any other man's view. Dostoevsky may be, as Camus claims, the prophet of the new religion of atheism and socialism, but Dostoevsky did not welcome or champion this development.

Dostoevsky's reply to the devastating indictments he has Ivan express occurs throughout the novel, but especially in the account of the Russian monk, Father Zossima. As Nathan Rosen points out, Dostoevsky himself saw Ivan's indictments and the account of the monk as *pro* and *contra* on this issue. [12] This novel should be understood, I believe, as an elaborate thought experiment, in which the natural consequences of various views and ways of life are shown in the life developments and life movements of the various characters. [13]

The question of the genuineness of sainthood is not answered philosophically, but with the living example of Father Zossima. We see his virtue by observing his life, teaching, and activity. His saintly example is contrasted with Father Ferapont, who possesses the trappings of genuine religion (fierce asceticism, fervent prayer, wearing chains under his robes to mortify his flesh), but who nevertheless spreads discord and dissenson among the monks. Ferapont represents, I think, Dostoevsky's admission that some religion is indefensible—religion of forms and trappings and even personal sacrifice without the essential heart.

Dostoevsky presents many things from Zossima's life and from the lives of the other characters that reply to Ivan's indictments. For example, Zossima gives three stories about his life before his conversion—the story of his brother Markel, the story of a duel, and the story of a murderer's confession. Each story contains an element of mystery, which suggests that all human life has a mysterious dimension encompassing the mysteries of faith, conversion, and cosmic justice.

Zossima tells the story of Job, but he ignores Job's claims about his innocence, focusing instead on the fact that Job's lost children were later replaced, and on the mystery that the new children erased the pain of the earlier loss from Job's memory. This is an indirect answer to Ivan's concern about the suffering of children.

Although accorded the status of a saint by the common people, Zossima neither mocks them nor is obsequious toward them, but merely serves them with dignity, giving blessings and counsel, thereby contributing to their genuine well-being. As a man of religion and tradition, he embodies what is best in life and contrasts dramatically with the lives of other irreligious characters, especially the Karamazovs.

Zossima brings together Karamazov, the father, with his sons, so that the father's buffoonery and despicableness temporarily subside. Yet the meeting is ultimately unsuccessful; Zossima is a saint, but he does not work miracles beyond the responsibility of others who meet with him.

Zossima recommends that Alyosha leave the monastery and marry, a recommendation that highlights the contrast between Ivan's troubles with the women in his life and Alyosha's lack of trouble. Ivan cannot achieve intimacy for any extended time, but Zossima sees intimacy as part of Alyosha's salvation.

Zossima's faith, though simple and elemental, is neither uneducated nor blockheaded. He lives it with good humor and good feeling for all, and he spreads goodness to all who will accept it. This contrasts with the gloom and nervousness Ivan spreads to his companions.

When Zossima dies, his body decays and begins to smell, denying to others the supernatural miracle they had expected. But a greater miracle happens, in that Alyosha and Grushenka go through several stages of inner transformation, culminating in the "Cana of Galilee" episode. Zossima brings the true miracle of inner change of heart; this miracle comes when one follows true insight and prefers doing good to doing evil.

Despite Mitya Karamazov's passion, his hatred of his father, his need for money, and his vow to kill his father (he even has the opportunity and the weapon), Mitya runs away from the temptation to parricide. If the Grand Inquisitor were right, these psychological and material causes should have compelled him to the deed. But every reader realizes the genuineness of his refusal and his self-restraint. His example shows that people have the inner capacity to overcome those forces.

Ivan goes away profoundly depressed after reciting his tale to Alyosha, and finally recognizes that this depression is caused by the revolting familiarity and impiousness of Smerdyakov. Even though Ivan hates his father and would like to see him dead, Smerdyakov's lack of piety toward the father grates on Ivan. Also, Ivan himself confesses complicity in the murder in the end, even though this is irrational and ridiculous because he knows no one will believe him. So even Ivan operates by a different ethic than the one he expressed earlier.

Ivan goes mad in the end, while those who follow the way of life of Father Zossima undergo inner transformation to a higher state of consciousness and way of life. Rebellion leads to psychological, social, and even physical degradation.

The atheistic socialism that Dostoevsky and Camus see (correctly, I believe) as the alternative to the religious view does not solve the problem of justice, but in fact ultimately promotes much greater injustice, even in the economic realm where it is supposed to be paramount. We have observed this dramatically in the last decades. So rebellion in the name of justice does not work even for its own ends.

By all these means (and others), then, Dostoevsky has presented an answer to the existential problem I mentioned above; he has shown both the consequences of that rebellion and an alternative to it, and he has presented all this in the form of an elaborate thought experiment.

By his own work of art, especially through the contrast between Fathers Zossima and Ferapont, Dostoevsky answers my second question about art. Dostoevsky himself is not afraid to criticize religion in his art, but he does so on a religion-affirming basis. His art shows that true religion does away with the need for rebellion and, in fact, leads both to a superior art and the human well-being fostered by Father Zossima.

Conclusion

The accusations given against God seem persuasive and often accurate, so that it may seem that God cannot or should not be defended. But the alternative to alliance with God is rebellion, and that can lead to consequences worse than those that prompted the rebellion in the first place. It is accurate to say, I believe, that the *worst* evils of the twentieth century have been perpetrated by persons or movements that have been anti-God (even though monstrous evils have also been committed by people who asserted their faith and belief in God). So we must conclude that God's goodness is at least greater than the goodness of any person who presumes to base goodness on some human perception.

Religions are a different matter; some of them, or some elements from all of them, must be rejected as indefensible. I have not given any philosophical method for distinguishing between true and false religions (or saints), but I have suggested both that we can observe the differences by means of thought experiments, and that literature, drama, and film often constitute just such thought experiments. From a philosophical point of view, we could say that I opt for a kind of empirical absolutism on the metaethical level. Notice, however, that this does not imply conventionalism; conventions can also be examined and criticized by the thought experiment method that I advocate.

If Unification theology is right, then God is not responsible for the moral evils that befall us. Indeed, God does all that is possible to avoid them, but God is bound by the choices made by humans. The task, then, is to persuade humans to make the choices that will lead to human well-being. Those choices must conform to God's will and principle in order that goodness will result. Religions have the task of truly apprehending the divine will and purpose, and thus they must unite on a higher dimension than has heretofore occurred. How this might be accomplished is more than can be said in this paper, but (to state my faith) I suggest that Unification theology and practice have the best answer that now exists.

NOTES

1. Quoted in Jacques Barzun, *Darwin, Marx, Wagner,* (Garden City, N.Y.: Doubleday Anchor Books, 1958), 56.

2. C. G. Jung, and Aniela Jaffe, *Memories, Dreams, Reflections,* trans. Richard and Clara Winston (New York: Random House Vintage, 1965), 150–51.

3. The major Unification texts are *Divine Principle* (Washington, D.C.: The Holy Spirit Association for the Unification of World Christianity, 1973) and *Outline of the Principle: Level 4* (New York: The Holy Spirit Association for the Unification of World Christianity, 1980). Other useful works are: Young Oon

Kim, *Unification Theology* (New York: HSA-UWC, 1980); M. Darrol Bryant and Susan Hodges, eds., *Exploring Unification Theology,* 2nd ed. (New York: The Rose of Sharon Press, 1978); M. Darrol Bryant, ed., *Proceedings of the Virgin Islands' Seminar on Unification Theology* (New York: The Rose of Sharon Press, 1980); and Frank K. Flinn, ed., *Hermaneutics and Horizons: The Shape of the Future* (New York: The Rose of Sharon Press, 1982). This section of my paper owes a great deal also to an unpublished work on theodicy by Jonathan Wells. I will not give citations for my claims in this section because it is a summary of materials from chaps. 1 and 2 of *Divine Principle* and *Level 4.*

4. Unificationism thus holds to the view called *monogenesis,* the view that all of the human race came from one source and not from several sources. While this is a minority view, at least as I understand things, it is not an unknown or antiscientific view, and there is some scientific evidence for it. Unificationism does reject what we might call simpleminded Darwinism; it does not deny that species change occurred, but it holds that these changes required the input of some higher creative force (God's power) in order that they could come about. They did not happen merely because of material factors. Also, Unificationism holds to the existence of both angels and of a spiritual world, and holds that these have profound effects on the physical or material world. On the questions of Darwinism, species change, evolution, monogenesis and cell development, see the forthcoming work of Jonathan Wells.

5. Humans came to be "lower than the angels" only because of the fall. They are supposed to be above the angels and must regain that status in the process of restoration.

6. For an account of the Providence of Restoration see "Overview of the Principles of Restoration," chap. 8 of *Level 4,* or chaps. 3, 4, 5, 6 and Part II of *Divine Principle.*

7. Fyodor Dostoevsky, *The Brothers Karamazov,* ed. Ralph E. Matlaw and trans. Constance Garnett, (New York: W. W. Norton & Co., 1976). I have used the Norton Critical Edition of this novel, which contains various commentaries on the novel, including those by Camus and Rosen.

8. Ibid., 226.

9. Ibid.

10. Albert Camus, *The Rebel,* trans. Anthony Bower (New York: Knopf, 1956). The section of *The Rebel* dealing with *The Brothers Karamazov* is reprinted in the Norton Critical Edition, cited above. My citations are from that edition. 836–37.

11. Ibid., 836–39.

12. Nathan Rosen, "Style and Structure in *The Brothers Karamazov* (The Grand Inquisitor and the Russian Monk)" in *Russian Literature Triquarterly,* 1, (1971), 1, 352–65. Reprinted in the Norton Critical Edition cited above, 841–51.

13. In my view, many philosophical issues, especially issues of what Aristotle called practical wisdom—ethics, political theory, theories of art and creativity and so on—are handled much better in literature, drama and film than they are in philosophical discourses. I do not think that this means that I am advocat-

ing non-answers to those questions, but instead I hold that those issues are especially well presented by means of thought experiments, and that dramatic, novelistic, and filmic presentations are really exercises in thought experimentation of a particularly subtle and profound kind.

14. My favorite filmmaker is probably Luis Buñuel, who is known for his scathing and lurid attacks on religion in such films as *L'Age d'or, Nazarin, Simon of the Desert, Viridiana, The Milky Way, Tristana* and *The Discreet Charm of the Bourgeoisie*. Buñuel's attacks on religion need not be resisted by a devout believer—in fact they can be welcomed and even enjoyed—because they are attacks on something that is indeed false and deserving of scorn. Also, Buñuel's films express what François Truffaut once called essential for a successful film, "an idea of the world and an idea of cinema." (François Truffaut, "What do Critics Dream About" in *The Films in My Life,* trans. Leonard Mayhew (New York: Simon and Schuster, 1978), 6.) Buñuel is a great and powerful artist, one of the most "biting" of all; hardly any religious artists have the same gifts. But just because Buñuel's art rests on his hostility to religion does not mean that an equally biting art could not be structured on a God-affirming or religion-affirming basis. But such an art would need to recognize the culpability of much religiousness, as does Dostoevsky. Dostoevsky's practice is the strongest argument for the possibility of a nontrivial but pro-God art.

5

On Hearing God

FRANK R. HARRISON, III

Today we apparently live in a world of Babel containing many voices, not all of them intelligible.[1] Of the seemingly understandable ones, each voice calls out in its own tongue and in its own way, "Follow *me!*" They each exclaim "I am the Way, the Truth!" "*I* am your salvation," each assures us. And how each struggles for our worshipful attention! Some speak to us of power, others of wealth. A few loudly whisper for us to seek knowledge to gain control of the world. In this scenario other voices demand democratic treatment, not only at the voting polls, but in all manner of situations. They say no one, no thing, is intrinsically better than any other. Some voices insist on a radical pluralism at all levels of existence. Most urge us to seek the pleasures of this world only, for there are no other worlds, no other pleasures. They say we are bound to an inexorable and inextricable wheel of fate; we should "grab all the gusto" we can as the wheel flings us by. Still other voices clamor for us to reject such materialism, such pluralism, and to follow them— to Jonesboro. Truly little can be made of this pandemonium, this cacophony. One thing appears assured, however. The voice of the God of Abraham, of the Apostles, and of the Church is not heard in this racket of our world, unless perhaps God's is one of the unintelligible sounds continually beating against our ears. What has become of the *Vox Dei* at one time so clearly heard by so many? Is it, as Amos once bemoaned, that God no longer speaks to us? Or is it, perchance, that God is continually speaking out but that for various idolatrous reasons we do not hear him?

Calling Out

This essay explores the thesis that God is continually speaking to us, but it is we who are not listening to him. Indeed, I shall argue that insofar as we continually prostrate ourselves before the idols of the world and the market place—the voices of Babel—we are incapable of hearing God no matter what he may be saying. And while God is not threatened by our idolatry, nonetheless we thereby set a limit to what he can meaningfully say to us. We set such a limit precisely because of limits we impose on ourselves of what it is possible for us to hear and to understand. Like the paranoid, no matter what is said or done by God, we weave it into an interpretation fitting our own view of the world—of whatever idol we hear, follow, and worship.

The exploration of my thesis that God is continually speaking out to us serves as an attempted defense of God. To suggest that the God of Abraham, the Apostles, and the Church is in need of defense is, on the face of it, odd. For what type of defense does God require? Certainly not a defense against either force or criticism. He cannot be assailed by these, nor his purposes thwarted. But idolatry is another matter. Falling down and worshipping before the idols of Babel, we can neither hear nor understand the God who is continually speaking to us. Therefore, God's specific purpose of calling us to himself is thwarted as is his more general purpose of maximizing-order-in-variety limited.

Not all of the particular tongues of Babel can be set forth and discussed in one essay. Nor even could all of the various choruses of such voices which, in one fashion or another, we often hear and worship in our lives as we dwell in the market place, the factory, the board room of business, the halls of academe, the laboratory, and in the church itself. So I select only one example, but one which is pervasive and prevailing in all areas of our life. While only one instance out of many, nevertheless a discussion of this idol will serve as a powerful example of a subsidiary thesis in this essay; namely, how we view our knowledge of the world of which we each are a part and how we view reality are both necessary determinants in whether we are able to hear God or not, and of whether we are able to speak of him or not.

In the remaining sections of this paper, I shall first present a sketch of a particular idolatrous view of our knowledge of the world and reality. Then I shall contrast another position which allows us not only to hear God and to act in God's image, but which also permits us better to understand and develop both science and technology. Unfortunately the limitations of space in this paper prevent me from spelling out the details and thus substantiating this broad claim. This must be left for another day. However, in this paper the foundations are laid for bringing together into one conceptual view of the world, and the relation of a person in it, both the voice of God and the very human activities of science and technology.

False Idols

In the contemporary technological world, now spreading over all parts of Gaia, there is a particular view of our knowledge of the world and of reality which has been developing since the times of the pre-Socratics. Above all, according to this idol, knowledge must be objective. And what of this objectivity? First, the factuality of the content of a particular claim of knowledge, that is, the actuality of what is claimed to be the case, does not rest upon either who, or what, makes or made the proclamation of knowledge. Many individuals and many societies have proclaimed such and such to be beyond doubt true (or beyond doubt false) only later to have been shown wrong. Rather, the factuality of the claim—the knowledge itself—is established by methods of observation, ratiocination, measurement, logical and functional coherence, consistency with other pieces of knowledge, and the like—by methods which may be followed by anyone. Second, the factuality of the content of any knowledge claim does not rest upon who, or what, receives it in whatsoever way. Indeed in this view of knowledge there is the essential commitment to the notion that factuality is to be identified with sensory perception of what is variable in the spatio-temporal order, even if the perception is "indirect." Nonetheless it does not matter whether you, I, or whosoever does the perceiving. In effect, the concept of *objective* functions in large part to eliminate any essential connection between the concepts *knowledge* and *particular knower.* In this sense knowledge, as objective, is viewed as impersonal.

Distinguishing between *knowledge* and *knowledge claims*—where *knowledge* is identified with *factuality* which is itself understood in terms of sensory perception of what is variable in the spatio-temporal order—the view under consideration holds that knowledge must be *certain.* Of course, while it is always logically possible to falsify any knowledge claim, useful claims ought to reach a very high degree of probability. While the concept of *logical possibility of falsification* is tolerable because it is part of the defining characteristics of the concept *knowledge claims,* empirical probability of such falsification is another matter. Indeed, the empirical probability of falsifying any really proficuous knowledge claim is to be close to zero. As there is a particular commitment underlying the notion of *objective,* so here also we find another essential commitment made by this view, namely, that the concept *knowledge* is primarily used in the sense of *perceptual knowledge.* For instance, the phrase "aesthetic knowledge" is logically odd, unless one means by it something to do with, say, art history, where "factual topics" of who painted what, when, where, and in which style are discussed.

Knowledge is also assumed in this view to be fundamentally both atomistic and independent. To grasp better this assumption it is helpful, if not necessary, to distinguish between *basic bits of knowledge,* (knowledge in its primary form), and *global knowledge,* (larger structures built up out of basic bits). The exact nature of such basic bits of knowledge is disputable. They may be taken to be isolated perceptions, or perhaps sense-data, or maybe independent neuron firings in the brain. The major restrictions in characterizing the basic bits are the assumptions that, primarily speaking, knowledge is perceptual knowledge, factuality is identified with sensory perception, and such basic knowledge is certain.

We have here what may aptly be called "Tinker Toy Epistemology." There are a great many basic bits—perchance even an infinite number of them—which may be put together in an indefinitely large variety of ways by externally imposing some forms, or patterns, on them. Now it is important to note that each basic bit is, in and of itself, both quite independent of any other basic bit and is also context-free. Each basic bit of knowledge stands, as it were, alone and without surroundings or background. Each basic bit is entirely in and of itself. Thus, from any particular basic bit of knowledge nothing follows, nor is any particular basic bit derivable simply from another basic bit. Certainly inferences can be made and structures constructed, but only when various grids, usually in the form of arbitrarily contrived rules, are externally imposed on sundry basic bits of knowledge. In this way, global knowledge is said to be created, or constructed, depending on one's philosophic or scientific bent.

How are the basic bits of knowledge reached? By analysis. Any global knowledge is nothing more than a collection of various basic bits of knowledge put together by means of some rules or other. By a method of analysis, global knowledge may be broken down into its parts. When this is accomplished, both the basic bits of knowledge and the rules relating them are displayed, and there is nothing more to understand of the global knowledge in question. From this stance, the concept of *systems analysis* is essential in the current prevailing concept of *knowledge*.

Finally, for the purposes of this essay, the only value any knowledge—basic bits or global—can have is instrumental. The sole value of any knowledge is its use in prediction, control, and in order to get something done. In particular, all knowledge is value-free in any sense of intrinsic value or of any purposeful action other than instrumental. Some knowledge—there is also worthless knowledge—may be useful as a tool in performing some task, in getting some job done. But other than in such situations as these, knowledge is valueless. In fact the concept *intrinsic value* and its corollary *purposeful action* tend to disappear altogether from this entire approach to knowledge and reality.

It is not surprising that the concept of *knowledge* I am displaying has a parallel in the concept of *reality*. To indicate this concept, all that it is necessary to do is to emphasize the concept *fact* instead of *knowledge*. Here facts are taken to be objective, certain, atomistic, independent, reached by analysis, and value-free. To the contemporary ear, all of this sounds "scientific." Yet I think that we should be reminded of a curious haze in our story which may now be brought into better focus. In that factuality, being a fact, is identified in some way or another with sensory perception, and in that some one thing is perceiving or could perceive, and in that no two things could ever have the very same sensory perception (all commitments made in and about these concepts *knowledge* and *reality* being discussed) then one is always on the brink of some form of nihilism and/or solipsism. Maintaining these concepts *knowledge* and *reality,* I am being driven to say that I am the only standard for what is to count as knowledge and that I am the only existing thing! But what are we now to make of our former discussions of *objectivity* and *subjectivity,* or *certainty,* or *method holding independently of any particular knower?* May we begin to suspect that we are being betrayed by a false idol? May it be that in this view *knowledge* and *reality,* in their own terms, are logically odd—are *contradictory?*

Given these concepts of *knowledge* and *reality,* by means of which we (presumably) see and hear ourselves and that world in which we dwell, how could God speak to us, explain himself to us, defend his ways to us—in general, make himself known uniquely as God to us? What defense, logically speaking, could God offer of his ways to man?

I presume that, in part at least, the Divinity would be speaking out in defense of his divine purposes and his goals and overall plans for his universe, of which humanity is but a part. Presumably these goals would be valuable in some sense other than simply instrumental, for in the case of the Christian God—the stance we have been assuming—what other ends could there be but the fulfillment of God's purposes? Yet, if God is to defend, that is to explain, himself by making known and justifying his divine plans for his universe, then logically speaking there could be no defense, no explanation within the concepts of *knowledge* and *reality* discussed above. Any fact which God could cite in his defense, anything God could tell us which we could possibly hear, would simply be about another fact in the universe. And even from many basic bits of such knowledge, we could make no inferences concerning the Divinity and his plans. Further since it is unimportant who, or what, proclaims knowledge or cites facts, then what could God, uniquely as God, say to us that we could hear? No knowledge, no fact, could possibly be uniquely related to the Divinity in such an essential way that we could do no other than view it as forming an explanation of his purposes to us. Even assuming that God is omnipotent in some sense of force and/or intellect, still, if we are committed to the concepts of *knowledge* and *reality* outlined in this section, there is nothing that we can hear God, as God, say to explain himself to us. Or if I, or you, do claim to hear God speaking in his own defense, such a claim is taken as merely a matter of subjective opinion and not the heard Word of God. Given the above concepts of *knowledge* and *reality,* while God is always speaking and acting in his own defense, we, because of our "intellectual filters," can neither hear nor see. Here the fault lies not with God but with us. Indeed it is we who have lost the Word of God. It is we who cannot hear him. It is not God who has lost his voice, who has chosen for now not to speak out.

Furthermore we really cannot put aside the suggestion that the above suggested idols of *knowledge* and *reality* harbor deep-seated contradictions. Indeed, in this situation we are rather like the paranoid. We hear and see what we do, or do not hear and see, because of our frames of interpretation of the world. Of course, one can take such comparisons only so far. Yet permit me to move one step further. Sometimes in therapy a paranoid person is brought to a position of appreciating his particular form of illness not by citing "facts" to him, not by pointing out what other people "actually do" or "actually do not do." Indeed, such moves as these are more often than not self-defeating. Rather with patience and persuasive measures of various sorts, the paranoid comes to see for himself that there is something fundamentally odd, in his own terms, with the way he views the world. Even so, once having seen this for himself, the paranoid may still tenaciously cling to his old ways until something more satisfactory can be offered to him which he can internalize as his own. In this section of this essay I have attempted to show that there is something fundamentally odd, in its own terms, with a certain commonly enough found view of knowledge and reality. Now I shall begin to suggest other concepts, an alternate approach, which over time we may develop, adopt, and internalize; and thus, we may finally cure ourselves of our own deafness to the Eternal Word of God.

An Alternative Approach

I have suggested that there are several core elements of some widespread concepts of *knowledge* and *reality* which, when taken in concert, lead to curious, if not contradictory, consequences. Not only are these views logically odd in their end results—for instance, the concepts of *objectivity* and *impersonal* leading us toward nihilism and solipsism—but they are also extremely limited, and limiting, in accounting for a very rich expanse of meaningful human experience and activity. Of course, other central commitments are that knowledge is perceptual knowledge, factuality is identified with sensory perception, and basic knowledge is certain. Yet such commitments in and of themselves lead us to ignore, or even to castigate, the responses of the human being to, say, concerns of religion, morality, aesthetics—indeed, to all basic questions of non-instrumental values and purposeful actions.

With these results before us, it is appropriate to turn to the far more difficult task of suggesting an alternative approach. In any attempt to provide an alternative approach to the epistemological and ontological stances I have outlined, it is not sufficient to offer a view which would seemingly do justice to religion, morality, and aesthetics, while at the same moment ignoring the great human activities of—and high success in—science and technology. Selective ignoring of various areas of experience in order to better explain other areas always leads to its own frustration. We must always strive to keep man's total experience in our vision as it has unfolded through communities of individuals over the centuries of their histories, and as it is even now manifesting itself. For only such a circumjacent vision as this will help to safeguard us from falling into some form of narrow-minded bigotry that we then call "The Truth."

There are four central concepts which I am going to introduce and discuss synoptically: Reality, World, Nexus of a World, and Person. I do not attempt to rigorously define any of these concepts. Indeed, I view them somewhat like logical primitives in terms of which everything else is "definable," but which themselves are "undefinable" within the "system" of which they are the primitives. And, as I proceed, I shall suggest corollary concepts such as *factuality, knowledge,* and *value* in terms of my four central ones. So I only present suggestions—pointers for what I hope you may come to see. And while what I shall suggest is not, in many ways, Socratic, nonetheless, I do wish to begin advancing a view of *knowledge* and *reality* that may serve as a means whereby one may hope to become wise and thereby be happy—a view in which wisdom takes precedence over (but does not deny) power, and happiness supersedes pleasure but does not term it "sinful."

The first of these central concepts is Reality. We may focus this concept by such phrases as "the given," "permanent possibilities of becoming," and "permanent possibilities of experience." Reality is that which I "bump into" and "rub across" continuously, which begins to become particularized and concrete out of various primordial experiences of it. And even though physical imagery is used here, I do not mean to characterize the notion of Reality only in terms of "physical things in the spatio-temporal order." I also psychologically, emotionally, intellectually "bump into" and "rub across" Reality. Sometimes these encounters are painful, sometimes pleasant. In most cases they are neither, but are simply amorphously there to be experienced and, hence, particularized under certain conditions. Even though I "bump into" Reality continuously in numerous primordial experiences, nonetheless Reality is what there is irrespective of me. To use the language of a metaphysician, Reality exists in and of itself, independently of any knowing mind, as a field of permanent possibilities of becoming and experience.

My second central concept is World. By World I understand the possibility of an ordered selection of various ongoing primordial experiences of Reality such that these primordial experiences are interpretable through a system of signs, thus becoming concrete and particularized experiences. Hence primordial experience is understood as an awareness of Reality by a sign interpreter such that this awareness is not yet expressed in a system of signs. And by *sign* I simply mean anything which can stand for something for some interpreter. Experience, then, is primordial experience of Reality made concrete and particularized, through the use of some system of signs, and of the signs through which primordial experience is expressed. The corollary concept *factuality* may now be understood as the possibility of expressing something about various experiences in a system of signs. By a sign interpreter interacting with Reality and expressing this ongoing interaction through some system of signs, a particular world and its various facts are being established. And it is important to notice that I do not say a particular world is being constructed. I do not construct my world; I establish it.

How is it that from the permanent possibilities of experience and becoming that various primordial experiences are selected to be brought into concrete awareness in the process of establishing a World and its facts while others are not? Indeed, a vast amount of selection is occurring here. While Reality may be conceived as a field of permanent possibilities of becoming and experience, not all of these possibilities reach factuality, much less being a fact. Nonetheless, Reality is experienced and Worlds are being established along with the facts of those Worlds—Worlds and facts which display great degrees of both variety and similarity. The bases for this selection, for the similarities and differences of Worlds, rests in certain "gestalts" coupled with "generic codes" every sign user possesses and brings to primordial experiences of Reality. These considerations point toward my third central concept, Nexus of a World.

By Nexus of a World I mean those elements necessary for the ordered selection of various primordial experiences to be brought into focus—to be particularized—in the establishing of a World, and necessary for the development and use of various system of signs in which facts are set forth. The Nexus of a World is that through which the multitudinous and various primordial experiences of Reality are interpreted and permanent possibilities of experience and becoming are actually selected and made concrete by means of a system of signs in a particular World. To express anything is always to discriminate. Of course, while I may discriminate between A and B, it does not follow that I "create" or "construct" A or B. However, though a process of such discriminations of what is there independently of the process of discrimination, namely Reality, a World is being established. Whatever is expressed is an interpretation of primordial experiences of Reality or other experiences which requires some context; that is, which is expressible only within, or against, the background of some Nexus. Since anything expressible always requires some Nexus against which, or within which, it is expressed, the total Nexus of a given system of signs can never be expressed, as it were, all at once within that system of signs. Nevertheless, various areas of any Nexus may be brought into focus at a given time, while later they become part of the background against which something else is expressed. In general, though, there are always those areas of a Nexus that are not expressible at a given time of overtly expressing something within some system of signs. Nonetheless, the very possibility for sign expression depends on this unexpressible background.

To this point, I have spoken only of sign users—beings who can use one thing to stand for something else. However, there are beings, such as humans, who use not only signs but also symbols. A *symbol* is understood as a linguistic sign. I shall leave the concept of *language* as intuitive except for the following remarks. A language is an ordered set of symbols related in various ways to one another, to the user, and to what, upon certain occasions of usage, they may refer. Within language the user may reflect upon the symbols he uses, their various relations, himself as user, and to what these symbols refer if they are being used referentially. A user of only signs cannot do this. For instance a sunflower may show it is dry by curling and yellowing leaves. A sunflower cannot, however, reflect upon the qualitative state of its dryness. It cannot say "I am dry." On the other hand, a human may show the Nexus of the World in which he dwells through his actions. He may also reflect upon it— talk about it. Let us, for a moment, follow this example.

To say something at all in a system of symbols, we must also experience the surrounding context of our speaking. We, as humans, each have a Nexus which is a necessary condition for using symbols. Now, the Nexus we each have is partly common and relatively permanent to all of us, and partly idiosyncratic and varied to each of us. As humans we are all organisms of more or less the same sort. And while we may not wish to defend an "eternal form" or "unchanging essence" as *human,* nonetheless, whatever our differences of race, particular physical appearance and behavior, or nationality are, we all belong to what can quite meaningfully be called the "family of humankind." We are, after all, neither ants nor dogs—although as humans we have more similarities with ants or dogs than with, say, sunflowers. But there are even fewer similarities between humans and rocks than between humans and sunflowers. In any event, humankind forms a community founded in an enormity of similarities in our organic nature; that is, humans are based in some permanent possibilities of becoming and experience of which we have primordial experiences, and which enter into the actual make-up of what we experience and call in our World "our bodies." There are also differences in our world views—the Nexus which I bring to my primordial experiences and which you bring to yours. Each of us is born into various societies and a particular time in human history. We each live within various governments and ideologies, and we each undergo various forms of education. Each of us, as the organism we are, is acculturated into a World established before our birth but taken up and modified by each of us. And so our Nexus is partially instantiated by the organisms we are, and partially by the acculturation we acquire. Nor are these facets independent of one another. The limits of the types of acculturation we may internalize are set, in part, by the type of organisms we are. But the organisms we are also change over periods of time because of acculturation. As an example of this, think of various dietary habits affecting organic changes.

My fourth central concept is Person. To begin, by Person I mean an intersection of Reality, World, and Nexus of a World which can be self-reflexive of this intersection and its various elements. Thus the concept Person is not identifiable with Reality only, or with something expressed within a World as a fact, or with a Nexus of a World only. Yet all of these are necessary elements of Person. Nor is the concept Person identified only with the ability, and activity, through the uses of some Nexus, to establish a World out of various permanent possibilities and differing experiences of which the person is himself a part. Presumably ants, dogs, sunflowers, and perhaps even some machines can do this. The concept Person includes all of these features. Yet it also includes the notion of self-reflexivity on these features. In this sense, a person is not only aware of a particular Nexus, but is also able, at least in part, to evaluate, reject, and change various areas of it. A person, unlike a dog, is able to introduce novelty into a World and to consciously produce real change. As a self-reflexive intersection of Reality, World, and Nexus, a person is at least to some degree self-establishing. To the extent a person is able to establish himself and his World, he is responsible and accountable for both the self and the World he does establish. And while I say his self and his World, both self and World are, as I have already stressed, shared—communal. Even so, there is great room for both variety and novelty.

In order to explicate more fully the central concept Person, the corollary concept *knowledge* must be introduced. For, as I understand the concept Person, a key characteristic of being a person is that such an individual has knowledge as well as experience. By *knowledge* I mean the expression of, in a system of symbols, the permanent possibilities of becoming and experience, as those permanent possibilities, that is Reality, are established in various particular ways in a given World.

Since knowledge is what is expressed in a system of symbols, and individual persons are users of symbols, my concept *knowledge* presupposes the concept Person as a knower. That is, by *knower* is meant a self-reflexive interpreter of various permanent possibilities of experience and becoming in the establishing of a World by means of some Nexus. But what is required is an individual knower and not a knower-in-general. For the concept Person involves, among other things, Nexus of a World, which has both its (relatively) permanent aspects and variable aspects. These variable aspects of a Nexus are part of the individuality of the person who knows this or that. In this sense, I wish to hold that all knowledge is personal.

All knowledge is the expression, in a system of symbols, of the permanent possibilities of becoming and experience as Reality is established in various particular ways in a given World. Nonetheless there are several aspects of knowledge which may be brought into focus for particular purposes at particular times in a system of symbols. Then other aspects of knowledge become part of the background necessary for the focusing of that aspect being emphasized. For instance, in that Reality is the permanent possibilities of becoming and experience, *metaphysical knowledge* may be stressed. Metaphysical knowledge is the expression in some system of symbols of what is permanent in any possible World—your World, my World, Worlds yet unestablished. If, on the other hand, various particular facts of a particular World are stressed, empirical knowledge is being brought into focus. Or one may wish to emphasize the establishing of a World out of the permanent possibilities of experience and becoming by means of a Nexus. In such cases axiological knowledge is being underscored.

In the second section of this essay, a particular and widely accepted concept of *empirical knowledge* is seen to be identified with *perceptual knowledge*. Furthermore, *perceptual knowledge* is closely aligned with concepts such as *sensory perception* of the spatio-temporal order, *objective,* and *certain.* Having already touched upon *sensory perception* and *objective,* I turn to the concept *certain.* In that the concept *certain* means something like "beyond any logically possible doubt" or "the denial of which would produce a contradiction," and in that *perceptual knowledge* is considered to be solely of the variable aspects of the spatio-temporal order, it is logically impossible to speak meaningfully of certain perceptual knowledge. Thus epistemic searches for what can be "empirically known with certainty"—immediate sensory perceptions, sense-data, etc.—are all utterly misguided. Instead of employing the concept *certain,* I wish to speak of the *certitude* of empirical knowledge. By *certitude* I wish to suggest that empirical knowledge is defensible and justifiable within various Worlds established out of Reality by some Nexus. In this essay I do not have the space necessary to explore my concept *certitude,* except to suggest that a defense and justification of empirical knowledge require an appeal to both order and value. Empirical knowledge viewed as having only pragmatic, or instrumental, value cannot in the last analysis be defended or justified. The successful pragmatic use of such knowledge remains completely mysterious forever.

To flesh out further the concept Person, I wish to elaborate the concept *intrinsic value*—a concept conspicuously absent in the widespread concepts *knowledge* and *reality* discussed in Section II. First, let me suggest a rather likely candidate for that which is valuable in itself and upon which every other sort of value is ultimately dependent. This is the value of the *optimizing-of-order-in-variety.* Note I do not say creating-order-out-of-variety, in which case the more order one has, the less variety. I do not wish to identify intrinsic value with either order or variety only. Intrinsic value is the optimizing-of-order-in-variety. Now, the degree to which order is optimized in variety is itself variable—in some cases more, in other cases, less. Exploring the suggestion that intrinsic value is the optimizing-of-order-in-variety, we also notice that intrinsic value is a process of some sort, namely, an optimizing process. As such, intrinsic value is not identifiable with Reality, nor a World, nor a Nexus. However, the intersections of these are identifiable with intrinsic value, for it is at these points that order is being optimized in variety; that is, Worlds are being established out of the permanent possibilities of becoming and experience. Here I am speaking of sign users in general and persons in particular. For while all sign users are centers of intrinsic value, that is, are capable to some degree of optimizing-order-in-variety, nonetheless the characteristic of self-reflexivity, to the extent which it is present in a person, permits a greater degree of optimizing-order-in-variety.

The God of Abraham, the Apostles, and the Church

Thus far, relatively little has been said concerning God. Indeed, I have carefully avoided arguing either for or against any particular theology or story concerning divine matters. Instead I have noted that some world views, such as the one presented in the section entitled "False Idols," prohibit our ever hearing God. On the other hand, in the preceeding third section I have offered a view which allows an understanding not only of God but also of science and ordinary matters-of-fact in our daily lives. Certainly I have not spelled out the claims of Section III in any detail, for this paper is not the place to do that. Even so, I wish to close my essay with a possible concrete application of the position presented in Section III to one theological issue.

There is one person who is supremely valuable in an intrinsic sense. That person is God. For in the person of the Divinity there is the greatest possible degree of optimizing order in an infinite field of permanent possibilities or experience and becoming. Indeed, Genesis 1:1–2:4a may be read in light of this supposition. God, the person, creates the void which is without form. That is to say, the void is the maximization of variety. In this sense, the void of Genesis may be identified with Reality or the permanent possibilities of all experience and becoming. Through the Divine Logos, that is, the Nexus of the Divinity, God is continually establishing the universe, his World, as the optimizing-of-order-in-variety. We, as human persons, experience or hear God through his creation of Reality, of which we are both a part and have primordial experiences, and through his showing forth his Divine Logos in optimizing-order-in-variety. For God, as person, is a user of symbols, and through his symbols God is continually speaking out to us. Since every symbol is also a sign, what may be used as a symbol by one person may be seen as a sign by another. Furthermore, while a person uses a particular system of symbols, that person is distinct from the symbols he uses. The symbols used by God to speak to us are simply those of his universe, which we, as parts, may interpret, misinterpret, or simply ignore through our own uses of signs and symbols. Indeed, an overarching theme of my paper is that given the certain concepts *knowledge* and *reality* we are forced to ignore God's symbols as being his in speaking to us. We cannot hear God speaking to us in our World because, given our Nexus, we cannot interpret his symbols. Indeed, we cannot even imagine the universe in terms of the natural language of God if we commit ourselves to the view of *knowledge* and *reality* outlined in the section "False Idols."

The above interpretation of Genesis may be pressed further. In Genesis 1:26 we read of God making (establishing) man in God's own image. What may we make of this? Let us understand the term "image" in the sense of "function." Then the suggestion of Genesis 1:26 is that we, as persons, are established to function like God. We as human persons are called upon continually to perform on a much smaller scale, and in much narrower confines, the very same work God is performing. We are called upon continually to optimize-order-in-variety in the Worlds we establish. To grasp this is to hear God speak to us in a defensible way of his plans and actions. Of course, we as particular individuals may not be very good "images" of God. Yet we cannot seriously attribute our shortcomings to God. For even though through our primordial experiences of Reality we "bump into" God in one of his aspects—the creator of all permanent possibilities of experience and becoming—still it is *we* who, in part, establish our own selves and our own World within which we dwell. And this is, in large part, our responsibility. Sometimes the Nexus we adopt—also in large part our responsibility—is such that it precludes us from bringing our primordial experiences into expressible forms in which God can be a part of our factuality. In this way we are quite well able to hinder God's work of optimizing-order-in-variety—of bringing intrinsic value into our World. Even though God may be omnipotent, we are still able to thwart, or hinder, his great work in our World. We are able of our own accord not to hear God. We may select to filter his voice out of our World. But far more important is it to be a good servant of our Master and his work. For to be a good and faithful servant is to share in the nature of God to the extent that we are faithful. Often it requires a good deal of courage to be God's faithful servant. We have to strive against tremendous distractions—many of which we ourselves establish in our World—while attempting to optimize-order-in-variety in our own life and in those around us. Nonetheless, to do this is to afford us a degree of happiness in this life based on optimizing-order-in-variety, even if at the cost of losing some short-term pleasures based on optimizing variety only. But far more important still is this: As faithful servants helping to establish the work of God in our World, we are afforded the justifiable and defensible hope for immortality in that we become more like the Divinity we aid.

—Ad majorem glorium Dei—

======================= **NOTES** =======================

1. I especially wish to thank both Professor William Power (Department of Religion, University of Georgia, Athens, Georgia) and Professor David Lochhead (Vancouver School of Theology, Vancouver, British Columbia, Canada) for their careful reading of and penetrating comments concerning earlier drafts of this paper. Their generous help and guidance are reflected in the better parts of my essay.

6

The Argument of Repression
JÖRG SALAQUARDA

While there have been many *types* of criticism of religion and, of course, still more *individual* philosophers, sociologists, psychologists, etc., who have criticized religion, the *set of arguments* they have raised against religion as such, or against certain religious ideas, is rather limited.[1] The same arguments recur time and again in the pertinent writings. They typically involve indictments concerning anthropomorphism, wishful thinking, immorality, hostility against sciences and studies, misuse of language, the existence of evil, the problem of freedom, and repression.

In the course of history, these arguments did not remain exactly the same, it is true; they were altered, augmented, corrected, stated anew—and it has been by no means indifferent in what time and in the context of which theory they were brought forth. Thus, all these arguments have run through a development, and it is interesting as well as rewarding to reconstruct the main stages of such a process. In the present paper, I shall try to do this for the argument of repression.

The method of my presentation is historical as well as systematic. On the one hand, I do not intend to "invent" versions of the argument, but I shall look for them in positions that were actually held. On the other hand, it would be boring to collect and analyze *all* doctrines or books which, at some time, have made use of the argument. Thus, I shall discuss only the ones that promoted a new and better version. And I shall prefer authors who come as close as possible to the ideal type of a certain version of the argument.

In general, the argument of repression claims that religious propositions are *imperatives* brought forth to cause people to behave in a certain way which is probably opposed to their real intentions. This claim does not necessarily include the assertion that religious propositions as such are senseless, i.e., that they do not refer to any objects. While the argument seems to make sense only if, at the same time, the notions of a God who exists as an independent being or of a transcendent realm are rejected, it is also compatible with the suggestion that religious ideas have an anthropological meaning and that religious propositions refer to real objects.

Even by this first and general description of the argument, it may easily be seen that by its own force and without being aided by other arguments, the repression-argument is not able to challenge the objectivity of religion as such. For its kernel is the repressive *function* of religious ideas and propositions, i.e., the way they are *used* in social life. Logically speaking, this does not allow for any consequences regarding the objects to which these ideas or propositions refer. That the ideas of hell or purgatory, for example, are repressive or at least in many cases are used in a repressive way has no consequence whatsoever for the actual existence or non-existence of hell or purgatory.

Nevertheless, the argument has gained great importance, especially during the last two centuries. In my opinion, this is due above all to its moral meaning. Repressive ideas or ideas which are often used to frighten others are rejected because they oppose emancipation. Thus, the problems we have to pay attention to in dealing with our argument are: What is meant by "repression" and by "emancipation?" Is it true that religious ideas favor repression and interfere with emancipation? Is it true for all religious ideas, or only for some of them, or only for a certain use of them?

As far as I can see, up to now three different versions of the argument have been offered. I shall discuss them in the following pages.

Clerical Deception

The first version might be called "repression by clerical deception." It seems that the first one to raise this version was Critias, one of Athens' thirty tyrants and, like his nephew Plato, a student of Socrates. In one of the very few fragments that are left of his writings, we find a story that starts with a report about a first legislation by which human society was founded.[2] According to that report, up to then there had been no religion because no need for it existed. But after the legislation, crafty persons cunningly invented the idea of God and some connected ideas in order to cause the mass of their fellow human beings to obey the laws. The crucial point is the fiction that there is a superhuman being before whom no action can remain hidden and who is able and willing to punish trespassers.

We do not know if Critias himself held this view. The fragment is part of a satyr-play on Sisyphus, who is, according to Greek mythology, the most cunning of all human beings. The idea of the play might be that Sisyphus, by this report on the origin of religion, is tempting the mortals just as once he had tempted the immortals and had been cruelly punished by them. Critias at least must have considered the possibility that all religious ideas were fictions deliberately invented to repress people, thus making rule over them easier.

In antiquity and in the Middle Ages, the argument was widely known; but in spite of that, it did not play an important role. Many an author stated it, but nobody seemed to take pains in discussing it. Take, for instance, the way in which Lactantius, one of the early Latin fathers, rendered the argument:

... conscience greatly checks men, if we believe that we are living in the sight of God; if we realize that not only what we do is seen from above, but also that what we think or say is heard by God.[3]

Then Lactantius quotes our argument:

And it is of value to believe this, as some think, not for the sake of truth but of utility, since laws cannot punish the conscience, unless some terror impends from above to restrain sins.[4]

Finally, the theologian comments:

Then, all religion is false and divinity does not exist at all, but all things have been confected by wise men in order that life may be more upright and innocent.[5]

Lactantius does not ascribe the argument of repression to certain philosophers or heretics. The "some people" he vaguely refers to may have been skeptics or Epicureans.[6] It is not known that at this time anybody really held the argument, even if some persons were suspected.

For our discussion of the argument, the following point is crucial: Lactantius does not reject the argument in general, but only the conclusion that God is a mere fiction. For he himself is interested in what we might call the "disciplinary function" of the idea of God. He is convinced that it is necessary and justified to threaten people with God and with divine punishment because in the absence of God they would not respect law. For Lactantius:

> . . . whether you draw kindness away from God, or wrath, or both, of necessity religion is taken away without which the life of man is filled with foolishness, crime and enormity.[7]

Lactantius argued, and many people up to now argue in the same way, that society could not exist without the idea of a God who will reward the good and punish the bad.[8] But in spite of that, neither he nor they accepted the argument of repression, because they were convinced that there is a real God. Some ideas of God or other religious ideas may be nothing other than fictions, but at least one idea is right insofar as it refers to the real, existing God.[9] Thus Lactantius and his like confirm what I have pointed out in general above: the (alleged or actual) repressive use of some religious ideas cannot challenge their objectivity. As long as those who believe in God are interested in the "disciplinary function" of religious ideas, they will not totally reject the argument, but, on the contrary, turn it against (alleged or actual) atheists. Lactantius may once more serve as an example. His book, *De ira Dei,* argues mainly against Epicurus and his followers, according to whom God does not care at all about human affairs. For Lactantius this thesis amounts to a denial of God's existence; because a God who does not love the good and is not angered by the bad, who does not punish, redeem, help, etc., is no God at all.

While this may be regarded as an agreeable argument, at least as far as the "God of faith" is concerned, it obviously does not prove anything about the existence of one God, or Gods. All it may prove is that it is incompatible with the notion of God that he does not care about human affairs. As long as atheism is not regarded as a debatable hypothesis, this is sufficient to reject the argument: an idea of God which was suspected to lead to atheistic consequences was unbearable.

The conviction that there is and must be a God was not seriously challenged before the second half of the eighteenth century. As long as there were no sufficient explanations of natural processes by science, and of human behavior by social science, only very few people could imagine the world functioning without God's help on the theoretical level; and even the most learned did not dare to live without the "disciplinary function" of the belief in God on the practical level. No wonder, then, that the argument of repression did not play an important role before the French Enlightenment when, for the first time in Western history, some philosophers and scientists openly "confessed" their atheism. For them—La Mettrie, Diderot and some of his colleagues who contributed to the *Encyclopèdie,* above all Holbach—the argument of repression became crucial. This was due mainly to historical and sociological reasons. France, at that time, was ruled by absolute monarchs who claimed to derive their powers from God. The church provided an ideological backing for this claim. Priests and theologians fiercely fought the fundamental ideas of the Enlightenment, which may be summed up in the claim for emancipation. In this fight they unscrupulously made use of religious ideas in order to keep the mass of the people in a state of dependence and to secure their own influence.

Against that background, Holbach, in many articles of his anonymously published *Pocket Theology,* described religious ideas ironically in order to point out their social and political intentions.[10] According to him, the ideas do not refer to any real objects but are simply instruments of repression in the hands of clergy and noblemen. I shall quote only two striking examples:

"*Innate ideas*—Concepts which nurses and priests have been teaching us so early, and have repeated so often that, when grown-ups, we believe to have held them from times immemorial or to have conceived them from birth. Obviously all ideas of catechism are innate ideas.[11]

God—Synonym for priest and, if you want, the *factotum* of theologians . . . The honor of God is the arrogance of priests; the will of God the priest's will. Who offends God offends the priest. To believe in God means to believe in what the priests tell about Him. If you are told that God is angry it means that the priests are out of temper. When theology replaces the word *God* by the word *priest,* it becomes the most simple of all studies.[12]

Though there is much irony in these "definitions," Holbach is undoubtedly serious. Here, for the first time in Western history, not only is the objectivity of some particular idea of God rejected, but also the objectivity of all of them. And since in eighteenth-century France the *philosophes* experienced religion, above all, as repressive, the argument of repression became for them one of foremost importance. The "reality" to which religious ideas refer is but the claim of dominance raised by noblemen and clergy. All religious ideas have been deliberately invented in order to support and maintain this claim. Therefore, in this "hypothesis of clerical deception," as it may be called, the first version of the argument of repression is not only stated or described but really held. This gives us the opportunity to enter into a short examination of its cogency.

To begin with what may be said in its favor—there can be no doubt that the argument becomes intelligible to a certain point when seen against the background of the actual history of pre-revolutionary France. Indeed, in this period most, if not all, religious ideas were used for repressive purposes. Holbach and his friends could provide examples galore of what they criticized. This observation may be generalized: Wherever and whenever religious ideas are used to secure the dominance of one group of human beings over another, they are rightly criticized by the repression-argument. Religion itself must be concerned that its ideas do not degenerate in the hands of unscrupulous and irreligious people.[13]

However, the promoters of the argument would not be satisfied by some such admission. Their goal is to unmask the repressive character of religion as such, and of *all* religious ideas. Since it was Holbach who stressed the argument in this way, he came as near as possible to the "ideal type" of its first version. The basic assumptions are still the same as they have been from the days of Critias: Religious ideas (a) are fictions; (b) are deliberately "invented" by a certain (small) group of people; and (c) serve as a rationale for the dominance of some human beings over others. What has changed is the framework. Holbach openly confessed his atheism and therefore was able to extend the argument to all religious ideas, including *all* ideas of God. Two thousand years after Critias, Holbach did not remarkably alter the argument but was presumably the first to hold it without reservations.

Now, what should be said about this version of the argument, apart from its possible value for the self-criticism of believers? Not very much, in my opinion. For (a) is not more than a corollary of a presupposed atheism; (b) is, most probably, wrong; and (c) is, at least, not generally true. I shall discuss these three judgments in more detail.

First, the argument does not and, of course, cannot prove that religious ideas have no real objects. On the contrary, in this version of the argument, atheism and the fictitious character of all religious ideas are presupposed. For to plea for an abolition of religion because all religious ideas are repressive is meaningful only if there is no real object to whom they could refer.

Second, the "hypothesis of clerical deception," for historical as well as for psychological reasons, is not very convincing, to say the least. It would presuppose that (a) there have been human beings without religion in prehistory; (b) some of them deliberately "invented" religious ideas, above all the idea of a God who would punish wrongdoers; and (c) the vast majority, by and by, began to believe in these fictions—so much that they disregarded their own wishes and impulses in order to please the fictive Supreme Being.

But as far back as our knowledge reaches, we always find traces of a certain cult which must have been connected with religious ideas. Furthermore, the assumption of a "clerical deception" and of its acceptance by the betrayed ones is psychologically unwarranted. This hypothesis is exclusively rationalistic and neglects the emotional parts of the human psyche. If it is hard to believe that some people should "invent" such major ideas as God, or redemption, or Heaven, etc., and combine them into an impressive and coherent net of myths, for the sole reason that they wanted to dominate others, it is still harder to grasp that all the others should believe in the objectivity of fictitious ideas which heap so many problems on them. Later hypotheses, above all by depth-psychology, have done away with such naivety.

Third, while (a) is not proven at all but presupposed and (b) refers to alleged facts which may be criticized only indirectly because, if ever, they must have occurred long ago, (c) deals with facts that are open for empirical scrutiny. Religious ideas are said to be repressive in that they support and maintain the dominance of some people over others. While this seems to be true in some cases, in many others it is obviously not. It is most likely to become true whenever secular and religious leaders are in accordance and their ideologies back each other, that is, comparatively seldom. More often, religions, churches, denominations, and their believers hold other convictions and opinions than states, parties, political movements, and their followers do. It is not only in our time that people who have joined an opposition have done so primarily for some religious ideas they believe in.

To summarize, it may be said that the first version of the argument is rather ill-founded. What it claims comes out to be false more often than not; and the alleged facts it presupposes are, historically as well as psychologically, most improbable.

Historical Materialism

The first version of the argument fails, but the discussion may have indicated that some of its main features allow for an improvement. It may well be claimed that religious ideas are repressive without tracing them back to a "clerical deception." The repressive character of these ideas need not be interpreted in terms of exterior dominance. Finally, all these hypotheses are compatible not only with sheer atheism but also with a view of religious ideas referring to real objects, albeit other ones than the believers themselves are aware of.

A doctrine that has taken these considerations into account is *historical materialism,* in which the second version of the argument of repression has been worked out and stated best. But even before Marx and Engels another philosopher, Ludwig Feuerbach, following some basic assumptions of German idealism, came out with an interpretation of religion which became important for the improvement of our argument. According to Feuerbach, the object of the central religious ideas is not God but man; they do not refer to a heavenly world but to this world and the lives of human beings.[14] This is to say that religious ideas are not regarded as false or fictitious but as true ideas which represent their objects in an estranged way.

"Man," in Feuerbach's doctrine, does not mean the individual human being, but humankind, or the essence of human. God, then, is nothing else than the essence of human; God's omniscience means the knowledge of humankind which is or at least seems to be infinite; God's love for humankind represents the love of one human being for another; sin means the estrangement of the individual from his or her true human nature; and redemption points to a kind of reconciliation.

Religious consciousness is, therefore, a disguised or estranged form of human self-consciousness. Religious ideas refer to the human essence, but the believers who hold them do not realize that fact; that is, they take their own human essence as another, superhuman being—as God. The difference from Holbach's view is obvious. While the latter understood God as a fictitious projection, and propositions about God as disguised imperatives only, God is a real being for Feuerbach, and propositions about God make sense, albeit they have no theological but an anthropological meaning.

This short overview may render it intelligible that Feuerbach himself did not use the argument of repression. He never fought religion but only theology and speculative philosophy which, in his view, imputed a false meaning to religious ideas. Especially in their Christian form, he thought, these ideas were generally true when interpreted in terms of their original anthropological meaning.

But Marx, though he built on Feuerbach's doctrine, revived the argument of repression and stated it in a new and more sophisticated version. He agreed with Feuerbach, in that religious ideas refer to humankind and to nothing else. But he was not satisfied with his forerunner's suggestion that religious ideas, on the whole, are right. To him, they are not, and one of the main reasons why he held that opinion involved the repressive character of religion.

To understand Marx's revival and improvement of the repression-argument, we must recall his anthropology. Man, for Marx, is primarily the "working animal." He is not human by nature; he has to make himself human by (social) labor. His human essence, there-fore, is not given but has to be achieved, now and again, by his own efforts.

Marx's view includes two consequences which are important for our study. Being a product of human labor, human essence (a) is not limited to man as such but comprises the whole world of man, that is, state, society, mode of production, civilization, etc.; and (b) does not remain the same throughout history but is changing along with the world man lives in. While Marx agrees with Feuerbach in regarding religious consciousness as a form of self-consciousness, for him this means neither that religious consciousness is fundamentally valid nor that it remains the same throughout history. On the background of Marxian anthropology, one has to ask *which* world of man and *what* stage of development are represented by certain ideas of God, or other religious ideas. For Marx himself they represent a perverted, estranged world characterized by class-struggle. He writes:

This state, this society, produce religion, *a reversed world-consciousness,* because they are *a reversed world.* Religion . . . is *the fantastic realization* of the human essence because the *human essence* has no true reality.[15]

Religious ideas, according to this doctrine, are spontaneous projec-tions of human beings who, unfortunately, are forced to live and work in an inhumane world. Their religious ideas (often) are correct representations of their human essences, but since these are not yet true human essences the ideas are, in fact, repressive.

All these considerations may be summed up in Marx's famous dictum that religion is "the opium of the people." Not only for

Feuerbach but for Marx, too, religious ideas are not "invented" by members of the ruling class in order to suppress the mass of the people. They are, on the contrary, unconsciously developed by the suppressed themselves who, by these ideas, represent to themselves their estranged human essences in an estranged world. But since religious ideas refer to a kingdom *to come,* to a redemption in a *heavenly world,* to a cancellation of alienation in another world, their effect may be compared to that of drugs—they further quietism, prevent people from bringing about a change in this world, and insofar are repressive.

This may be sufficient to collect the fundamental features of the second version of our argument. It claims that religious ideas (a) do not refer to God and the Heavenly World but to the suppressed themselves; and (b) are a kind of drug which helps the mass of the people to endure and survive in an inhumane world.

No doubt this version of the argument is, in some respects, better founded than the first one. Furthermore, it is embedded in a cohesive doctrine. Some of the most striking shortcomings of the hypothesis of "clerical deception" are eliminated. No longer is religious consciousness regarded as false and fictitious but is acknowledged as self-consciousness, albeit in an estranged form. The "invention" of the religious ideas is replaced by the much more intelligible hypothesis that these ideas are products of a spontaneous self-deception. And no longer are religious ideas charged for aiming at stabilizing a secular order, but for achieving, and maintaining a (detrimental) inner stability of the estranged individual in an estranged world. Again I shall turn now to a short examination of the argument.

First, while I regard Feuerbach's and Marx's doctrines that religious consciousness is an estranged self-consciousness as much more convincing than Holbach's view, it is obvious that this doctrine, too, does not depend on the repression-argument. The second version of the argument presupposes the anthropological interpretation of God and his realm just as the first was based on the denial of God. For if there should exist a God apart from the essence of man, not all ideas of God could be reduced to this essence, regardless of whether they were used in a repressive way or not.

Second, if religious ideas have their origins in the psyches of the suppressed, there is no need to explain that these people believe in them. In this respect, Marx's doctrine is coherent. But even if we remain within the framework of this theory, another point may be doubted, namely, that *only* the suppressed should develop religious ideas.

If suppression is an outcome of class struggle and reflects the antagonistic contradictions of class societies, the above stated assumption would suggest that before and after class societies there have been or will be societies without religion. This agrees with the Marxist hope that religion will vanish in future communist societies. On the other hand, according to this view, as long as a given society is decisively influenced by class dominion, religion cannot fade away.

It is, of course, not so easy to confront the Marxist theory with empirical objections because admittedly, up to now, there has been no real communist society and we do not know too much about the society alleged to exist before the beginning of class struggle. But in both cases evidence rather seems to be against the Marxist assumptions. As already stated above, cult and religion seem to belong to *all* states of human development. And the increase of atheism in East *and* West is most likely due more to the development of science and technology, which both have in common, than to the different organizations of society.

Third, religious ideas are said to function like drugs—they enable estranged people to live in an estranged world. These images of a better world serve a dual purpose. On the one hand, they console those who are exploited by others; but on the other hand, they prevent them from fighting for a better life in this world.

While this, too, is a better and psychologically more convincing hypothesis than Holbach's, it is, in my opinion, nevertheless the weakest part of this version of the argument. It is true that the "opium" of religion can be used by a ruling class as a drug *for* the people only if it has been the drug *of* the people before. But is religion really the "opium of the people" and nothing else? Of course not! Religious ideas have inspired all great movements of emancipation. Ideas such as the common suffering of all creatures in Buddhism, of sharya in Islam, of the kingdom of God in Judaism and Christianity, and many others have provoked those who believed in them to fight for a better life in this world, too.

A modern Marxist philosopher, Ernst Bloch, has stressed this aspect of religion,[16] and the same is true of Erich Fromm.[17] Both of them reject "repressive religion" or "religion of the masters" but acknowledge an "emancipating religion" or "religion of the suppressed." If we take into account the use people have actually made of their religious convictions, they were certainly right. And it might be added that, in most cases, religious ideas may not be neatly divided into either repressive or liberating ideas; rather one and the same idea may be used in a more repressive or in a more liberating way.

Thus the argument of repression, once more, becomes a *discrimination* between different types of religion and not a weapon against religion as such. This view has succeeded in historical materialism itself. Consider, for example, the following lines from a Marxist reader:

The classical authors of Marxism-Leninism as well as Marxist-Leninist parties have always, very precisely, distinguished between reactionary powers which misused Christian religion to justify the domination of capitalist private property, of exploitation, of profit, and of war; and those believers who favored the fight for freedom, democracy, and social progress and who thus became potential allies of the working class. [18]

It is not the intention of this text to recommend Christian or other religious ideas. Neither were Bloch or Fromm devout Christians. But their distinctions make clear that the argument of repression fails even in its most sophisticated version, if it aims at *all* of religion. Religion is obviously not the repressive part of culture—at some times and in some traditions it may be, but in other times and other traditions it plainly may be the most progressive part. And, on the other hand, there is presumably no idea of any social impact which may not become repressive, not even the ideas of revolution or emancipation themselves.

Self-Control

If we may characterize the second version of our argument by the catchword "opium," we could use "self-control" for the third one. Its protagonist is Friedrich Nietzsche, and some important aspects of it are found also in the criticism of Sigmund Freud. A major distinction between the third and second versions is that not only the suppressed but all human beings develop religious ideas which, since they have a necessary function for man as such, cannot be replaced simply by changing the social conditions.

To make this third version of the repression-argument intelligible, it will be best to start with a sketch of Nietzsche's hypothesis on the genesis of conscience. Nietzsche's starting point was Darwin's theory of the origin of species, even if he did not agree with the Englishman in many respects. In the second essay of his *On the Genealogy of Morals,* Nietzsche tried to reconstruct the conditions of anthropogenesis, i.e., the situation which forced our "semi-animal" forefathers to become human.[19] It must have been " . . . the most fundamental change . . . [man] has ever experienced," comparable only to " . . . the situation that faced sea animals when they were compelled to become land animals or perish."

Under the pressure of socialization, the "semi-animals" were forced to change their impulses and drives or give them another direction. This is Nietzsche's decisive thought on man's becoming human; instead of living out their instincts, people learned to turn them against themselves. Two decades before Freud, Nietzsche coined the word "internalization" (*Verinnerlichung*) to characterize this process, the outcome of which was the human soul. Man became a reflexive animal, the animal that was able to develop a civilization.

Nietzsche never tired of describing how much pain, suffering, and disgust this process of internalization brought about. It has been, so to say, a long process of suppression and repression which has ended in the internalization of the repressive powers: "bad conscience" or, more generally, conscience as such was established.

Freud's theories about the genesis of the "superego" widely resemble Nietzsche's genealogy of (bad) conscience. In his *Introductory Lectures on Psychoanalysis,* Freud mentions Kant's a priori theory about conscience, which he does not reject as one might presume. He acknowledges that the assumption of a divine origin of conscience makes sense, insofar as conscience does not belong to man's natural existence. Then he goes on to say:

. . . as it is well known, young children are amoral and possess no internal inhibitions against their impulses striving for pleasure. The part which is later on taken by the superego is played to begin with by an external power, by parental authority. Parental influence governs the child by offering proofs of love and by threatening punishments which are signs to the child of loss of love and are bound to be feared on their own account. This realistic anxiety is the precursor of the later moral anxiety [*Gewissensangst*]. So long as it is dominant there is no need to talk of a super-ego and of conscience. It is only subsequently that the secondary situation develops (which we are all too ready to regard as the normal one), where the external restraint is internalized and the super-ego takes the place of the parental agency and observes, directs and threatens the ego in exactly the same way as earlier the parents did with the child.[20]

Freud thinks that each individual runs through the same process by which in the course of anthropogenesis the species has gained its human features. One of them involves the super-ego, which partly suppresses the impulses and partly directs them in socially acknowledged lines.

For Nietzsche as well as for Freud, religious ideas have played an important if not decisive role in this development. Both authors agree with Feuerbach and Marx that religious ideas are spontaneous projections and refer to man himself, to his life and world. However, according to their views, not only the suppressed but all men develop a conscience or super-ego and consequently a religion. Thus they, too, presuppose a state of development in which there is no religion—but they regard it a pre-human state. Only when man is ruled, at least to a certain extent, by his own conscience can he be called human. This is not so clear in Freud, but Nietzsche's late writings provide many examples. The most impressive one is in the third essay of his *Genealogy,* where Nietzsche portrayed the "ascetic priest" as a person who has already succeeded in internalizing all exterior commands.[21] Therefore, the ascetic priest no longer obeys anybody other than himself. But since he is not used to such a situation, he is unable to understand that it is he himself who exerts control over his impulses. Thus, he interprets the call of his conscience as the call of God, his own commands as those of a superior being.

In comparison to other people, the ascetic priest has accumulated an enormous amount of power; and by appealing to a God, he becomes even stronger. This makes him superior to those who cannot, at least up to now could not, achieve full internalization— superior to those who would vacillate between the claims of their (weak) consciences, the desires of their impulses, and the rules imposed on them by others. These "weak people," or "slaves," as Nietzsche drastically used to call them, are attracted by the power and decisiveness of ascetic priests. In their eyes not only God but the ascetic priests themselves are hardly human. They begin to model their ideas of God after the image of the priest.

According to Nietzsche, religious ideas have still another function in this development. Being the "shepherd" of the weak, the ascetic priest is confronted with those who have not yet internalized the cultural demands at all and continue to live as "semi-animals." He cannot fight these "strong ones" by war and weapons, for in that they are his superiors. But he is more prudent than they are; and his most sophisticated and most effective weapons are—religious ideas. By them the ascetic priest succeeds in breaking the self-confidence of his enemies and gains, so to say, a hold in their own minds. Note the following lines from Nietzsche's *Twilight of the Idols,* where a former strong one is described who has been "improved" by priests. He now looks

> . . . like a caricature of a human being, like an abortion: he had become a 'sinner,' he was in a cage, one had imprisoned him behind nothing but sheer terrifying concepts. . . . There he lay now, sick, miserable, filled with ill will towards himself; full of hatred for the impulses toward life, full of suspicion of all that was still strong and happy. In short, a 'Christian'. . . .[22]

Freud, too, stresses the view that civilization in general has been paid for dearly. I need not discuss his widely known theory of sublimation in any detail. Suffice it to say that, according to him, the idea of God has been by far the most important means to achieve and maintain an inhibition of one's impulses.

Let us now compare this version of the repression-argument to the two other versions. Its characteristic features are: (a) the object of religious ideas is man as such, insofar as he is human and no longer animal-like, that is, insofar as he is able to exert a certain amount of self-control; (b) religious ideas are spontaneous projections of all human beings; their great variety is due to the different situations and to the different abilities and interests of men; and (c) religious ideas are primarily a means of achieving and maintaining self-control.

As far as (a) is concerned, the third version faces the same problem we have already discussed for the others. The argument does not offer any evidence that there is or can be no God, but it is based on that assumption. That *all* ideas of God, and the ideas connected with this central concept, are *nothing other* than projections of human power, as Nietzsche claimed, makes sense only if it is certain that there does not exist any God. The religious consciousness, by the way, need not deny the possibility of Gods who are projections of human power, but it would regard them as idols.

Points (b) and (c) above are closely related. I shall therefore discuss them together. Their main problem is a certain ambiguity which strikes everybody who tries to come to terms with Nietzsche's, and Freud's criticisms. Both authors fiercely criticize religious ideas and their repressive character and would prefer a world without religion. But at the same time, they point out the major role religion has played in the course of anthropogenesis. Especially Nietzsche links together the ability to exert self-control, humanity, and religion so closely that it is hard to grasp how one of the three could be taken away without doing away with the others, too. Thus, the arguments of the two critics are in accordance with the results of the history of religion, and are psychologically better founded than those of Feuerbach and Marx, but thereby they seem to support religion rather than to reject it.

Nietzsche himself seems to have been aware of this problem. He made two attempts to escape the consequences I have just pointed out. The first, more radical one aimed not only at transcending religion but also at transcending the man who cannot endure without religion as long as he remains human; this was an important aspect of Nietzsche's doctrine of the "superman" (or "overman") who was to replace man. The other attempt consisted in the distinction between at least two types of religion, that of the strong ones and that of the weak ones. Nietzsche, then, would accept the former and reject only the latter which, for him, was above all Christianity. Both attempts raise severe problems which I cannot discuss here. For us, the most important problem is that of anthropogenesis. Nietzsche, it seems to me, was not able to reconstruct a path to humanity which did not lead to the internalization of repression—and I think he was right in that.

To be a human being means being able to exert self-control, at least to a certain extent. In that regard, man is distinguished from animals, which are governed by their instincts, and from God who is in accordance with himself from eternity to eternity. This has been acknowledged by all philosophers and theologians, and all of them took into account this human condition in working out their anthropologies. It is a matter of semantics if we use the word "repression" here or not. For there is always something "in" man that is "repressed" by something else. You may call the one "impulse" and the other "reason" and agree with the dominance of the latter. Neither Nietzsche nor Freud denied that, but they wanted to make clear that there is no dominance without "repression."

To make the third version of the argument valid, its promoters had to prove that religious ideas favor a kind of self-control which is more repressive than is needed in order to become and remain human, or which is even exclusively repressive; while other ideas, such as scientific ones, would help to bring about a much better way of self-control which is not at odds with emancipation. But while Nietzsche and Freud helped to make obvious the problem of mastering oneself, without which man can neither become nor remain human, they could not prove that religious ideas as such are worse than others, or that these ideas did not establish a successful and liberating coordination of human powers.

Some Concluding Observations

To sum up, I would like to point out the importance of the argument of repression. In the long history of this argument, critics of religion succeeded in unmasking repressive structures in churches and societies, repressive religious ideas, and repressive uses of religious ideas. Everyone who believes in God, or adheres to a certain religion, should be aware of these problems and try to avoid them. The argument, therefore, has been and will remain an indispensable means of religious self-criticism. Furthermore, the argument helps us to understand social and psychical processes; it also offers valuable insights about the "human condition."

But, up to now, the argument could not give any evidence that there is no God, let alone that there cannot be any. Though the argument has been greatly improved in the course of history, even its most sophisticated version is based on the assumption that God does not exist as an independent being. Thus, it cannot, in turn, serve as evidence for such an assumption. The argument fails whenever it is intended to prove that *all* religious ideas are repressive, regardless of what meaning we give the word "repression" or in which theory we embed it.

NOTES

1. See K. H. Weger, ed., *Religionskritik von der Aufklärung bis zur Gegenwart* (Freiburg: Herder, 1979). This little dictionary discusses about one hundred critics of religion and the positions they hold.

2. See H. Diels, ed., *Die Fragmente der Vorsokratiker* (Hamburg: Rowohlt, 1957), 140 ff.

3. Lactantius *De ira Dei* 8, in Lactantius, *The Minor Works,* trans. Sister Mary Francis McDonald, O.P. (Washington, D.C.: The Catholic University of America Press, 1965), 74.

4. Ibid.

5. Ibid., 74–75.

6. Lactantius refers now and then to Cicero's *De natura deorum,* where similar arguments are raised against an Epicurean position.

7. Lactantius, 74.

8. Cf. Voltaire's famous dictum that one had to invent God if He did not exist—doubtlessly for disciplinary reasons.

9. Cf. Thomas Hobbes, *Leviathan,* chap. 12: ". . . some of the old Poets said, that the Gods were at first created by human Feare: which spoken of the Gods (that is to say, of the many Gods of the Gentiles) is very true."

10. *Théologie portative ou Dictionaire abrégé de la religion chrétienne,* pseudonymously published (par M. l'abbé Bernier, licencié en théologie), Londres, 1768.

11. Ibid. See the article entitled "Idees innees." The translation is mine.

12. Ibid. See the article entitled "Dieu." The translation is mine.

13. This is not to say that there could be no legitimate "disciplinary function" of religious ideas at all. But this is not my problem here. To deal with it would require a detailed theological discussion including the question of the so-called "third use of Law."

14. What is claimed here is true only for the position Feuerbach held in the first edition of *The Essence of Christianity,* 1841.

15. See Karl Marx, *Zur Kritik der Hegelschen Rechtsphilosophie: Einleitung.* The emphasis is Marx's. The translation is from Moscow: The Foreign Languages Publishing House, 1957.

16. See especially his *Das Prinzip Hoffnung* and *Atheismus im Christentum.*

17. See especially his *Psychoanalysis and Religion.*

18. *Einführung in den Dialektischen und Historischen Materialismus* (Berlin: 1977), 470. The translation is mine.

19. See the second section of Nietzsche's *On the Genealogy of Morals* ("'Guilt,' 'Bad Conscience,' and the Like"), in *Basic Writings of Nietzsche,* trans. and ed. with commentaries, Walter Kaufmann (New York: The Modern Library, 1968), 493 ff., 520.

20. Sigmund Freud, *The Complete Introductory Lectures on Psychoanalysis,* trans. and ed. James Strachey (London: George Allen and Unwin, Ltd., 1971), 526.

21. See the third section of Nietzsche's *On the Genealogy of Morals,* "What Is the Meaning of Ascetic Ideals?" in Kaufmann, 533 ff.

22. See the seventh section of Nietzsche's *Twilight of the Idols,* "The 'Improvers' of Mankind" trans. R. J. Hollingdale (Baltimore: Penguin Books, 1968), 56.

7

Judging Religion
MARTIN PROZESKY

The rise of secular lifestyles together with the increase of religious pluralism of many societies has made the problem of how to judge religion very real to many people. Some people have been raised as believers in the faith that dominates their culture, only to find concepts that they once regarded as the deepest truths losing their power and appeal in the face of the secular challenge to religion. Others grow up with no real spiritual allegiance but find, in their teens or adult life, that they desire some kind of faith but are perplexed, puzzled, and often put off by the invitation to commitment by different creeds, some of them confident of being the only true religion. Then there are people who retain membership in a particular faith while simultaneously sensing and responding to aspects, at the least, of others. And at the far ends of the spectrum, many either dismiss all religions except their own as inferior at best and false at worst, or reject all of them as cultural fossils from the lost age of faith. In each of these situations, judgments are made about particular religions, about parts of them, about secularism, or about religion in general. Those judgments are almost always highly subjective, and seldom is there any explicit awareness or application of relevant criteria according to which these judgments could objectively be made.

For some of us, eager to live responsible, rational, moral lives, this situation is simply not good enough. Confronted, let us say, with a Christian fundamentalist insisting on a Bible-based faith in Jesus as the only way to salvation, and a zealous Muslim equally emphatic that it is the Qur'an alone which reveals the true way to peace with God, we want our reactions to be based on defensible, objectively valid criteria, not on prejudice, cultural accident, emotional vulnerability or ignorance, however sincere and well-meant.

In this paper I explore a way of solving the problem. I argue that certain of our ordinary experiences provide guidelines which can be developed into two main criteria for judging religion, and that although our existing faiths *as usually interpreted* fail to meet them, at their core they nonetheless have the basis for a dramatic transformation which would meet those criteria, so qualifying for the whole-hearted (and wholeheaded!) support of the people whose interests this paper seeks to explore. And while such a transformation has an obvious religious importance, it might also be one of the few things that could safeguard our planet and its people from nuclear and environmental catastrophe, as I shall briefly explain near the end of this article.

The conclusions presented in this paper differ in three main ways from those reached by John Hick in his important article "On Grading Religions."[1] Whereas Hick does not consider it possible to apply rational tests to the central, originative religious experiences which underlie the great faiths, or to the great religio-cultural totalities that have developed from them, my own view is that rational and cognitive tests are in fact applicable. And whereas Hick's concern is with the great world religions, I am extending the exploration to include nonreligious views of reality alongside the great faiths as claimants for our support and agreement, so that we can evaluate religion with the secular alternatives also in mind. And finally, Hick's presentation of the great world religions, is, I think, revisionary in the sense that he sets them forth as effective soteriological movements in *each* of which people's lives are in fact transformed. I agree with this interpretation of religion, but I do not think it is typical of most believers in the various religions, who seem rather to think that only their own faith truly gives salvation/liberation, or is best at doing so, or is the unrecognized basis of any soteriological effectiveness present in other religions. And as I take up the problem of evaluating religions, it is their actual claims that I wish to assess and not a revised (and in my view very enlightened) picture of these religions.

These differences of approach and verdict are my main reasons for offering an additional contribution to this highly relevant, contemporary problem of what we might call the criteriology of religions.

The Standpoint of This Paper

What we see (or think) is often dependent on where we stand when we look. The standpoint adopted in this paper must therefore be made as clear as possible. It can be summarized in four points.

First, religious commitment must be publicly defensible on factual and rational grounds, because otherwise we have no way of protecting ourselves against error, delusion, and rank subjectivism. Faith should not be mainly the result of cultural accidents like being born into a devout family and society, of immature and ill-informed decisions, of gullibility, or of fears whipped up by dark warnings about hell and perdition. If we do make religious commitments, they should be the crown of our best learning and thinking, not alternatives to them.

Second, I assign greater importance to the discovery of knowledge and the global maximizing of well-being than to any existing religion or philosophy, so that I appraise the latter in the light or the former and *not* the other way around. I take this position because there is undeniable proof that up to this time religion has, in some respects, been an obstacle to the discovery of truth, for example in the conflict between Galileo and the Catholic Church over the nature of the heavenly bodies.

Third, I hold that we are *integrated* beings, so that the way we think and behave in our ordinary, everyday lives is also, basically, the way we function in the religious life, adjusted to meet the special characteristics of that life. We do not have one set of functions for secular life and another for religions; and faith, if well-founded, can be the fulfillment and not the negation of our human nature. Given this view, it is consistent to propose, as I do in due course, that criteria for judging religion can be derived from secular experience.

Fourth, this paper proceeds from the recognition that no religion (and indeed no secular world view) has in fact succeeded in establishing a commanding hold on the intellectual and moral loyalty of the human race. What we have are competitors for our allegiance in a contest which has, as yet, produced no victor. Therefore, the truth or falsity of basic religious claims is an objectively open question, concerning which inquirers are fully entitled to raise all the questions they can. In other words, the global religious situation with its claims and counterclaims calls at the present time for *evaluation* rather than defense or attack.

Concerning Religion

Turning now to religion, several of its characteristics need to be emphasized in the context of the present paper. These are: religion's sweeping, fundamental claims, and their importance for us if true;

and the ability of religion to evoke absolute dedication from multitudes of people. These characteristics appear to be shared by all the so-called world religions. In the central doctrines of these great spiritual movements, we find what purport to be the most basic truths about things in general, about what is supreme, and about who we really are and what could happen to us at the deepest and most enduring level of our existence. My concern here is not to list these claims but to draw attention to their nature as purported *fundamental* truths about reality. Closely related to this first characteristic is the second one, namely, the *momentous significance* of these claims for all people, because, if true, they reveal our own deepest nature and destiny, indicating what we must do if we would obtain supreme and ultimate well-being. Thus, religion functions as a disclosure of things that supposedly affect us more deeply and lastingly than any other kind. Small wonder, then, that there is a third, related, characteristic to be emphasized; namely, the way religion evokes in many people the total dedication we observe in the great prophets, martyrs, gurus, rabbis, mullahs, and evangelists, and also in their countless followers and fellow devotees. Faith for these people is a dedicated, wholehearted involvement in something much greater than just themselves—it is an orientation toward something which they insist is transcendent and supremely enriching. It evokes and is thought truly to merit the absolute commitment of the believer in a way no other form of life has been able to match consistently. This applies both to the great spiritual leaders as well as to the numberless hosts who have fought the good fight and kept the faith against any and every opposition including death itself.

And now, in the marketplace of religious claims and counterclaims, I ask if life, for the kind of contemporary, evidence-weighing person I have in mind, can validly exemplify such unreserved dedication without belying, shunning or deriding significant facts relevant to assessing religious assertions. These assertions purport to be the most important of all truths, affecting us more profoundly than any other. If true, we would be insane not to order our lives according to them at once. But instead of speaking with one voice, the world's prophets offer us different fundamental claims and different paths to salvation, while secularists denounce them all as mistaken. For some people the only reasonable way to deal with these competing calls for commitment is to examine them meticulously *before* accepting or declining, and indeed to keep open the possibility that the wisest policy, despite the apparent urgency of the issues involved, may be neither to accept nor to reject any of them at all. But without proper criteria with which to judge these competing creeds, none of this can happen. Let us proceed, then, to seek the necessary criteria.

Toward a Criteriology of Religions

Where might we find criteria with which to judge the issues placed before us by religion and its enemies? Many believers implicitly use their own religion as a norm, judging everything else in terms of it, so we might well consider this source first.

Could we satisfactorily use, say, Christianity as our criterion? While this is exactly what most Christians (and, *mutatis mutandis,* most other believers) do, it has at least two fatal problems. First, precisely *which* Christianity (or Islam, or Buddhism) is normative, since there is no single version to guide us? Those who assume that *their* personal faith is an adequate basis for making the assessments under discussion have merely begged the central question or simply failed to exhibit an awareness of it. It is *not* self-evident that Orthodox Judaism, or Advaita Hinduism, or any other faith, is the true faith by which others can validly be judged. And if it is not self-evident, then convincing, public grounds must be produced to prove the point. Yet this is precisely what believers have failed, hitherto, to produce. The reasoning, evidence-demanding adjudicator is thus justified in looking for something more than mere spiritual habit or assumption in the business of deciding what to believe.

The second objection to using any of the world's religions as a yardstick to judge the others is even more serious: it entirely exempts the allegedly normative religion from any real evaluation. How can we genuinely *judge* Catholic Christianity, for instance, if *all* we have to go by is what Catholicism alleges and does? Clearly it *must* pass such an evaluation, but the price is to deprive that so-called evaluation of any substance whatever. Moreover, it runs the risks of blinding us to possible flaws in the exempt religion and of misevaluating the virtues of other faiths.

These two objections seem to me to vitiate recourse to any religion as the proper source of criteria with which to judge the momentous issues set before us by prophets and skeptics. Equally, they also rule out any recourse to counterreligious philosophies, and for exactly the same reasons. If it is unacceptable for us to *presuppose* the fitness of, let us say, Eastern Orthodox Christianity as a norm by which to judge these matters, then it is also unacceptable to presuppose the suitability of Bertrand Russell or Karl Marx. So we shall have to go elsewhere. But where?

My suggestion is that we can derive the necessary criteria from analogous sectors of our ordinary experience. Religion, I have been at pains to emphasize, presents us with what allegedly matters most to us, so perhaps we can find guidance from situations in life which confront us with other deeply important issues.

Marriage is one instructive analogy because of the magnitude of the step being taken. Another is to enter the priesthood or ministry of a church. Then there is the decision to move with one's family to a new job in another country, or to take on a highly dangerous mission, or to play a prominent part in a campaign to achieve a goal, like women's liberation. These examples all involve highly significant steps on which a great deal will depend, often including the happiness of others. A few of them might be seen as among the biggest decisions most of us will ever take. Now since all of us try to take the *right* decision in such matters, there must, logically, be implicit or explicit criteria which we regard as appropriate to and workable in these situations. What are they? What makes the choice of a particular partner, country, job, or cause in life a *wise* (or foolish) choice in our own eyes and those of our friends?

I think there are three considerations in these situations. Decisions on matters like these are considered to be good (i.e., to be worthy of approval) by virtue, first, of the *greater happiness* for all who are affected; on the basis, second, of the most *thorough knowledge* of the situation; confirmed, third, by the agreement of relevant, competent third parties like our friends and relations, or any others who have our best interests at heart.

In examining the analogies mentioned above, it transpires that each of them conforms to this threefold pattern and that in unwise or wrong judgments one or more of the criteria in question is not met, particularly the need for very thorough knowledge. Readers are strongly encouraged to make this analysis for themselves and test its validity as rigorously as they can.

Before proceeding, we must, however, attend carefully to a fourth criterion which is seldom considered because in most situations it is met quite unconsciously *before* we apply the others, and this is that whatever we are evaluating must of course exist. Investing in bogus business offers or fake land deals are classic situations where this criterion is operative but has been neglected. So is mass public support for sociopolitical myths like Aryan racial superiority. In these examples people make important financial, personal, or national commitments to nonexistent things, deceived by persuasive persons more cunning or ruthless than themselves. Essentially there is failure to obtain the assurance that the company or land or ethnic status exists at all, and as such it could be treated as part of our guideline about thorough knowledge. But since the point does not affect most of my earlier examples, I prefer for the present to speak of a distinct, fourth guideline. When we come to the question of criteria for judging religion, this separation will not be needed, as we shall shortly see.

As for ventures which involve groups of people—for example, voters choosing a new political system—the same criteria appear to be at work in the way we think and act, except that when there is no unanimity the preference of the majority is, of course, usually accepted as binding on all who are involved. And it is fair to add that for individual and group alike, the more important the step being contemplated, the greater the need for extreme care in discovering and weighing all the relevant factors. We justifiably censure any lighthearted, precipitate, or ill-informed rushing into serious ventures; we rightly pity *and disapprove* of those who pay good money for nonexistent but persuasively advertised land, and, conversely, we rightly find ourselves irritated by people who take excessive pains about trivial decisions. Though seldom clearly aware of what we are doing, our reactions in these situations are made appropriate by adherence to the criteria identified above, which amount to a fully-informed agreement of those affected, or a majority of them, as to the greater happiness accruing from the proposed step for all concerned, or at least for most of them; and confirmation by the approval of knowledgeable, concerned third parties, provided always that what is at stake really exists.

When called upon to become a follower of Christ or the Buddha, or to forsake such leaders, the issue before us is admittedly more serious (if true) than any other, but this does not necessarily invalidate the criteria identified above. On the contrary, what else can guide us if we wish to manifest in our faith a responsibility not inferior to that which marks our best secular actions? But while these criteria should still, therefore, operate, there definitely is added pressure to apply them even more stringently because the stakes are higher still and the matter, involving the invisible order as it does, is more subtle. In particular, we must be sensitive to the possibility of acting deludedly when we make religious commitments, an accusation forcibly made by all materialist critics of religion. Those of us sympathetic to religion would be wise to consider this possibility most carefully, not just because it *is* a possibility, but also because not to do so is to ignore relevant considerations. No respectable religion would want to thrive on such criteriological irresponsibility. In circles dominated by people who were raised as and continue to be believers, it is especially important to place this matter high on the agenda, because hitherto it has almost always simply been ignored under the sheer pressure of these believers' consensus that God, or Brahman, or Sunyata, or Allah, obviously is real. Yet, for people outside such circles of spiritual consensus, those beliefs, as many of us know firsthand, are the very opposite: devoid of the reality alleged by the insider.

It is time now to crystallize the argument so far. To responsibly judge religious assertions and their related calls for our allegiance, we must ask the following questions, which embody the guidelines established above. *First,* can we be sure that whatever we are being invited to accept as supremely important to us really exists and is not merely a venerable illusion? *Second,* have we examined carefully, fairly, and thoroughly all the relevant information concerning the step being contemplated, particularly taking great care to hear alternative or opposing points of view? *Third,* can the proposed step reasonably be expected, in light of the facts established in the previous criterion, to engender greater benefit and happiness for *all* concerned than any other? If not we could scarcely be entitled to judge the step a worthy one, let alone supremely worthy. And *fourth,* do competent judges among those who have our best interests at heart agree with the verdict reached on the basis of the first three questions?

Such are the guidelines which emerge from our most important secular decisions and which, in the absence of noncircular religious criteria or of anything else that could guide us, are all we appear to have as we ponder the far-reaching but conflicting claims of religion and secularity, seeking for ourselves a reasonable, responsible way of responding to them. Let us see next what happens when they are applied to the various religions jointly, which I shall regard as patterns of life in which there is complete dedication to a transcendental realm of spirit as the ultimate reality and supreme source of goodness, wherein alone we can find perfect blessing.

Judging Religion

In applying these criteria to religion, we must first of all condense them somewhat. The first two belong together because the way to apply the former—concerning the objective existence or reality of the alleged spiritual dimension—is by applying the latter, which calls for meticulous examination of all relevant information. But whereas this would mean, in many situations, checking on the *nature* of the person, proposition, or property being considered, in religion it must first of all mean checking whether we are indeed in the realm of the real and not in delusion or error. Like the person reading about a persuasive land offer, we must first ensure that what the attractive photographs depict really is there for the investor. Thus the first two guidelines can be combined into what could be called a broadly cognitive criterion: are there adequate, objective grounds for concluding that the alleged supreme reality in fact exists?

It will be clear to many that most if not all religions will fail this first, cognitive test. Anyone who examines carefully and fairly all the relevant facts (the main ones being the very real disagreements among believers as to the nature of the supposed supreme reality, whether the Trinity, Allah, Yahweh, Brahman, Sunyata, or the Tao and so forth; their markedly different claims about the way to find salvation; the existence of secular people who are not less upright or intelligent than believers; and above all the absence of satisfactory ways of identifying any of these alleged spiritual realities) must, I think, concede that while it is possible that some such entity exists, we are *not* in a position to declare, objectively, that it does. Deeply held religious convictions of this kind abound, of course, but they appear almost always to be the result of other procedures than the kind of careful, objective, criteria-based assessment I hold to be desirable. In particular, as Hick rightly points out in the article already cited, the overwhelming majority of believers must acknowledge a significant degree of cultural accident in the determination of their convictions. And as we all know, those convictions tend to be implanted in the young or held by persons probably ignorant of the range of facts just mentioned, not to mention such factors as emotional vulnerability and group pressure. The plain conclusion is that most commitments to an alleged, supreme spiritual reality do not rest upon any judicious application of objective criteria, and any that do so rest have not been brought to the attention of those of us who seek guidance here. If we evaulate the various religious doctrines asserting the reality and describing the nature of a supreme spiritual entity by means of rigorous cognitive procedures found fruitful and workable in life's other major dilemmas, we simply will not reach a conclusive verdict either for or against those doctrines. Let me mention some prominent aspects of this process of cognitive judgment.

The materialist critique of religion and above all secular experience of authentic human life, which is every bit as saintly and caring (and sometimes a lot more open-minded) than traditional modes of religious existence, call in question the very reality of the realm of transcendent spirit of which believers speak, and they have *not* been convincingly refuted by believers. Historical criticism calls in question some fundamental religious tenets, such as incarnational literalism and divine creation, while philosophical criticism calls in question the coherence of other notions equally fundamental to many religions, such as the classical conception of God, Chalcedonian Christology, and the concept of divine action in history. According to the criterion of objective reality, it is clear that issues like this cannot, objectively, be the valid focus of absolute dedication or unconditional acceptance, at least until reservations about their reality and adequacy or truth are decisively met. Difficult as this may be for believers, they need to face the problem and admit the truth that on this issue—belief in a realm of spirit—their critics have exposed genuine shortcomings and problems, and that it is at least possible for secularism or materialism to be closer to the truth about reality than the concept of spirit or any other form of idealism. Moreover, modern cognitional analysis, with its doctrine of conceptual relativity, surely refutes the allegation of some traditional religions that their central beliefs are unrestrictedly and timelessly true and valid, or free from the conditioning effects of the cultures where they were formulated. Similarly, modern epistemology since Kant undermines confidence in the ability of our minds to discover, receive, or recognize perfect answers to ultimate questions, so invalidating all calls for unconditional and permanent acceptance of the classical beliefs of the various religions. In addition, the unescapable fact of direct contradictions among the religions regarding central tenets calls in question the adequacy of some and even all of those tenets, since they cannot all be true. For example, is the ultimate reality a personal, supreme being or not?

On grounds of realism and truth, the criticism of traditional religion is thus clearly justified in some very central respects. Secularists have, of course, not refuted believers, but they *have* shown that the case for religion is much less secure than believers suppose. Moreover, the evidence at my disposal indicates that in most religious contexts the catholicity and criticality of mind on which I am insisting are never demanded, often ignored, and sometimes even prevented by means of intellectual, social, and emotional pressures too strong for the majority of believers to resist. For example, in which spiritual tradition are adherents encouraged to investigate with the utmost rigor the fundamental tenets of that tradition itself? How many Christians are asked by the authorities of their own churches to examine and substantiate their assumptions about Christ and his goodness? More important, how many are helped to develop the intellectual and emotional resources needed for such an exercise? I have heard Muslims criticize biblical notions with a rigor that would be impressive if it were also applied to the Qur'an, and the same in reverse with Christians. Gotama's mental sophistication strikes me as exceptional, but it appears to have fallen short of a full, critical appraisal of the karmic world view so deeply embedded in the ancient Indian mind.

As these instances show, the actual record of religion in terms of rational justification appears to be far from satisfactory. But perhaps this need not necessarily be the case. Of this I am, however, somewhat skeptical. When traditional religious teaching has been exposed to rigorous, unfettered assessment, the result has often been to undermine it and force it to change, as has been the case with Galileo on cosmology; Darwin on creationism; Hume on miracles; Kant on natural theology and on the capacity of the mind; geology on the age of the earth; documentary criticism on the nature of the scriptures; religious pluralism on elitist and exclusivist doctrines; and latterly historical and philosophical criticisms on Chalcedonian Christology. People with the standpoint identified earlier in the paper cannot give unconditional loyalty to a system of existence whose proclaimed love of the truth so often turns out to be theoretical rather than practical, and which has often dismissed or scorned rather than answered its critics. Nor is it hard to find the root of this ill: it is the fatal error of assigning absolute status to unproven spiritual notions and then institutionally safeguarding them from proper scrutiny. So I am unable to conclude that religion hitherto meets the cognitive criterion before us.

But suppose for argument's sake that this first, cognitive criterion had in fact been passed by one or the other religion, so that we were able to conclude that there really is some kind of higher spiritual entity affecting us more deeply than anything else. Our next step would be to ask whether commitment to that entity really is a supremely worthy and moral step, as determined by the greater happiness it would engender for all concerned than would any alternative step. How does religion, as represented by the so-called world faiths, fare in regard to this question? My impression is that one of the greatest problems about virtually all definitions of religion is their metaphysical bias, whereby faith is construed merely as a form of ontology, for example as a perception of the ultimate reality or a relationship of absolute dependence on God.

However, once the religious life itself is carefully examined it quickly and globally transpires that faith always has another major component, namely, a quest for and taste of benefits flowing from that ultimate reality, typically expressed as a doctrine of salvation with accompanying ritual enactments. Through the ages the religions of the world have functioned as means of making available the greatest possible enrichments of our problematical and fretful condition. With this in mind the criterion of furnishing supreme happiness for all yields a more favorable verdict than the previous one, and the glory of religion up to now has been its success as a source of help and hope to suffering people.

Despite this, the verdict cannot be unconditional approval. The history of religion—theism, perhaps, in particular—often belies its own redemptive intentions, especially with regard to the here and now. The assessment of Christianity, for instance, in terms of the present criterion, must be rigorously open to the grim facts of its long toleration of slavery and continuing subjugation of women, its crusades and persecution of dissidents, its burning of witches and heretics, its cultural associations with nuclear madness, the worst wars in history and the perfecting and sanctioning of the politics of racism. Take, for instance, the custom of many theists, indeed of the majority, of devoting lavish buildings to the least needy, namely, the deity, in a world where most people are hungry. To think of Christianity as an unbroken succession of figures like Mother Theresa is to err gravely. It is not for me to find fault with the faith of others on this score, but to insist that all faiths be scrutinized for their achievements and failures as instruments of supremely life-enhancing effects here in this present life of ours. My suspicion, however, is that all the so-called world religions, with their common orientation to an order of reality supposedly higher and better than this physical one, will be found wanting in some measure so far as the enriching of the physical is concerned.

What about my third criterion, concerning the views of other competent judges? Much depends on how we define competence, but in the present context it must first be a matter of possessing thorough knowledge of the whole question of religion and secularity, coupled, secondly, with moral qualities we would admire, especially concern for and action on behalf of the happiness of others. Significantly, I do not find any consensus among people with these qualities concerning the validity and wholesomeness (or otherwise) of religion, and the same is probably true of others. When we find such lack of unanimity concerning the wisdom, for example, of accepting a new job offer, most of us would surely conclude that great care and hesitation were in order, and that there were probably important considerations both for *and* against the step. At the very least we would be quite clear, if our own investigations had not already made us so, that accepting the new job might turn out to be a mistake, all things considered, with greater prudence attaching to remaining where we already are. Why should religious commitments be exempt from such an eminently sensible and beneficial way of thinking and behaving? Surely it is more reasonable to hold the opposite view and treat religion in the same way, but even more carefully. After all, even in religion itself this policy is explicitly endorsed in at least one illuminating way. The Anglican service of marriage opens, in the words of the old Book of Common Prayer, with the admonition that the step the couple is about to take is not to be enterprised "unadvisedly, lightly and wantonly . . . but reverently, discreetly, advisedly and soberly. . . ."

Thus it is reasonable to conclude that the absence of consensus concerning the objective legitimacy or illegitimacy of fundamental religious commitments on the part of competent judges is itself a sign that all is perhaps not as well here as believers mostly assume nor, for that matter, as bad as skeptics in their turn are apt to suppose.

To summarize the discussion in the present section of the paper, it can be said that my proposed criteria call seriously into question the objective legitimacy of religious commitments *as hitherto interpreted*.

They would incline the kind of person whose standpoint I am exploring to withhold any verdict upon, and especially any absolute endorsement or rejection of, religious allegations concerning spiritual entities, while at the same time evoking admiration for the concern in our various religions for the greatest well-being of their adherents, even though the actual moral record of some faiths is clearly very blemished in certain respects. And from the differing examples of competent judges, such people would rightly infer additional grounds for withholding their commitment.

Now some believers might be inclined at this point to object to my criteria, branding them invalid or unworkable because no existing religion can pass them. In particular this might be alleged against my first criterion, which is clearly fundamental. I can understand why, subjectively, this reaction might be forthcoming from a dedicated believer. But it seems to me that the objection would depend, for any logical or objective force it could have, on a begging of the entire question of whether *any* religion is so secure on cognitive and moral grounds as to merit our wholehearted membership. If there were such a religion, it would make sense to reject criteria which fail it, for clearly that which fails a successful entity, or belies the truth, must be unsound. But it is precisely the existence of such a religion that is in doubt, and in these circumstances it is entirely possible that there is no such religion, all of them being in some measure defective. There is no logical or factual case for insisting that some religion or other *must* be valid; on the contrary, maybe the truth is that these venerable patterns of life are nonetheless ones that we must and will transcend as we sharpen, deepen, and broaden our minds, and as we recalibrate our moral sense. This being a possibility, there is nothing logically improper about setting norms which all religions would fail. The same is, of course, true of any anti- or nonreligious lifestyle, but I am not here dealing chiefly with them. So while the present criteriological proposals might yet turn out to be unsatisfactory, this can scarcely be *merely* because they work against prevailing religious commitments, though that may be difficult and even impossible for some very ardent believers to allow.

Thus, I find that procedures which are eminently reasonable and workable in other crucial dilemmas of life, and which are not self-evidently invalid concerning religion, generate the judgment that absolute religious commitments, *as hitherto construed,* cannot claim objective, public justification. People who are content with a purely private view of religion will not be bothered by this judgment, but very few believers hold that view, rightly seeing in it a fatal trivialization of what they hold to be more important to everybody than anything else. Furthermore, if spiritual commitment requires the type of behavior (i.e., a failure to act judiciously) which we rightly censure as irresponsible in every other context, is that perhaps not evidence that the fault lies with religion and not with my criteria? After all, we do not permit the very young to enter into legal contracts or other major undertakings, and we caution the ill-prepared against them at any age. But not so the undertakings of faith. It is at least possible that this is a matter for justifiable censure of current religious practice rather than of its critics.

I have not mentioned all that is relevant to this evaulation because the point is already made. Beyond doubt, our ancient ways of faith, wonderful and justified in their own heyday before modern times, do not meet the relevant criteria in question any more. Those who criticize religion have a point that we dare not dismiss. This could mean that the age of faith, like that of Ptolemaic cosmology, is now forever over for all who open their minds completely, and who demand that faith be compatible with objective intellectual and moral norms or be abandoned. But I prefer to explore the possibility that religion is in fact changing shape, though admittedly the change is evidently radical beyond anything in the history of religion, at least in the West.

If religion or faith is undergoing a dramatic change of shape rather than simply becoming obsolete, then it must be shown that total dedication to something greater than oneself—which is arguably the minimum definition of religion that could be sustained—is still legitimate. In other words, there must still be something we can *all* love wholeheartedly, serve unselfishly, and celebrate joyfully (as in traditional religion), while at the same time seeking the truth about reality openly, critically, and rigorously. There must be something real, true, universal, and of unsurpassed importance to which we can bind ourselves and set our hearts upon in the way made beautiful by the saints of the past in the East and West. I think there is such a potential focus of faith in our time.

Transforming Religion

I find the clue to this potential transformation of faith in a central human characteristic which has undiminished force in the ancient pathways of traditional religion, in secular experience, and in the strange hinterlands beyond both; and this is our universal human hunger for and experience of health, wholeness, healing, and happiness, as individuals and as communities—a hunger for the universal enjoyment of the supremely worthy. I should like to call the service of this ancient hunger simply the way of blessing for all the earth in the here and now. This is where the profile of a contemporary religious life, worthy of total commitment, can be found in our time, not as a refugee from its critical temper but as a practitioner and beneficiary of it. Let me sketch the main characteristics of such a faith.

In the first place, there would be an absolute dedication to the task of healing the wound in creation, as Alan Paton has called it, to promoting life, liberty, fulfillment, and well-being for all and opposing all harm-doing, exploitation, violence, and the conditions which encourage them. In this endangered planet, with its desperate sufferings and injustices, there is the most urgent need for people to take up as their main commitment the way of blessing in the here and now, instead of dogmatizing about the methods of obtaining perfect health beyond the grave. By doing so, believers would certainly meet the criteria of enhancing happiness for all and of realism. We all suffer, and we all long for relief. Often that relief depends entirely on somebody else, and so its provision reveals the unescapably social nature of our existence as interdependent beings. And all of us experience the happiness that comes, uniquely, from helping others, such as our children, our partners, or the needful strangers who lie by our waysides from time to time. Is there anything more real than this? Here, then, is a basis for faith and self-commitment which is a fundamental part of our very being as persons, dependent on no cultural, linguistic, or historical accident or particularity, and at the same time surpassingly important and real to us all.

Second, there would be *no* permanent attachment to any given view of reality or what might be ultimate about it, but only a provisional, experimental holding of whatever emerges from unfettered global inquiry as the closest to the truth. Only the goal of growth toward the truth would be unconditional. Belief in a realm of spirit might turn out to be the closest we can get, but I cannot see any justification for making it a condition of genuine religious life, let alone an absolute condition. Even more so with traditional theism. Neither can be established with the necessary certainty. The most that is valid here is to explore the viability of the concepts of spirit and God as symbols or metaphors about an issue upon which there can be no question of certainty, and hence no legitimate case for dogmatism or conversion, and no cause for combat with critics either.

A faith along these lines would exhibit intellectual qualities entirely consistent with the relativistic philosophy of mind noted in a previous section, and it would not be embarrassed by the conflicting ontological contentions of the various traditional religions. It would be tied to neither materialism nor supernaturalism, displaying instead an open naturalism that takes physical life with utmost seriousness without dogmatically asserting that it is the only kind of reality in which we participate. Structured in this way, the life of faith would always simultaneously be an experience of cognitive growth, capable of intellectual humility and self-correction and mercifully freed of the millstone carried by most traditional believers, namely, irrevocable allegiance to the merely tentative. One might argue that those who indulge in cognitive arrogance, such as claiming to identify the ultimate truth of things with perfect precision, deserve to be crushed by that millstone. But as one who has felt its dreadful weight and rejoiced at the blessing of its removal, I cannot share such a stance. The way of liberation from that impediment seems altogether more worthy and in keeping with the path of blessing. In any event, a religious life freed of cognitive absolutism would not only meet the criterion of rigorous, public, cognitive justification; it would thrive on it, ever ready to help and heal whatever the unfolding picture of reality reveals.

Thus, thirdly, there would be a self-critical, informed, and self-correcting stance on the part of transformed religionists who become conscious of the demands being made of them, sensitively but resolutely identifying core and husk in their heritage and reassigning priorities from the latter to the former. I have no doubt that this would involve pain, but that is better than dishonor, and it would certainly be worthwhile. Who would not wish to advance from being primarily an uncritical purveyor or imbiber of dubious and even defunct mythologies, to being primarily an instrument in the way of peace, learning, healing, and happiness for all?

These are only the fundamentals of the way of blessing. The details cannot be discussed now. It is more important to summarize how this way meets the criteria identified above. It would always be open to the truth. It would welcome all knowledge, however much it undermined earlier notions. It would be focused upon an un-doubted reality, namely, the sorrow and suffering of the earth at a time of unprecedented need, and the reality of healing, however incomplete. It would not make promises about the future, except the promise that if there is one, we wayfarers on the path of blessing will help and care in whatever way is needed. It is completely open to all and beneficial to all, and by the same token it is also of supreme importance. What better use can we make of ourselves than to be primarily and unreservedly on the side of healing, fellow workers in the cause of the greatest possible well-being for all? And thus the importance of our inherited styles of religious existence lies in their potential for changing into something like this, thereby meriting again the kind of total dedication we associate with spir-itual commitment.

Conclusion

Today we face the first chance in all of history to develop a planetary religious reality—to find the global amidst the deceptively regional, the supremely worthy amidst the relatively good, the jewel within the lotus. Here, amidst unprecedented global anxiety, the world seems to invite the energies of faith to a fresh outpouring, unclut-terd by the surplus baggage of the old days but faithful still to the ancient hunger for blessing and an abiding instrument for its provi-sion. So although my criteria are cold comfort for the old way of interpreting religion as an unshakable commitment to things we cannot prove, those same criteria, and the salvific core of religion as actually experienced, nonetheless leave us with the judgment that there is indeed at least the chance of a genuine religious life in our time and in the age ahead. The way to it is not by buttressing and prolonging spiritual provincialism or mythology masquerading as ultimate truth, but to begin, or perhaps resume, the way of blessing *here and now*. If there be an existence beyond this one, and if it be worth having, it will need no other preparation or qualification than this.

NOTES

1. John Hick, "On Grading Religions," *Religious Studies* 17 (1981): 451–67.

8

Perspectives on Creation and the Defense Of God

KLAUS A. ROHMANN

Apologia is generally known to be one of the earliest forms of Christian theology. From the very beginnings of Christianity, its believers were urged to proclaim their faith publicly and give an accounting of it. The following words of the first letter of St. Peter could be considered the Magna Charta of theology: "Be ready always to give an answer to every man that asketh you a reason for the hope that is in you . . ." (1 Pet. 3:15b). But who are those who ask Christians their reasons for hoping? One cannot exclude persons in juridical situations. In the Acts we read accounts of Christians who were forced to defend themselves in court. But the letter probably meant the situations of daily life above all, for its author specified that one has to be ready "always"; one must give an apologia "to every man that asketh." The person who asks may be a friend or an enemy. He or she may be a neighbor or a representative of the state, somebody seeking the causes of faith who is well on the way to believing already, or a person who is striving to do away with Christianity. Certainly not least of all, the one asking may be oneself. From the very first, Christians experienced the need to prove the credibility of their beliefs and to refute objections raised not only by enemies and by potential believers but by members of the Christian communities themselves.

Is the defense of God, therefore, the kernel of theology? The term defense sounds a bit negative and, as we shall see, quite different from the sense of the Greek apologia. Moreover, you will remember that the first letter of St. Peter bids us answer "with meekness and fear," with courtesy and respect. The New Testament concerns itself, and not only in this passage, with more than just the task of giving an apologia for the reason ("logos") of Christian faith and hope; it concerns itself also with the method by which an apologia can be given.[1] A very fine example is St. Paul's sermon in Athens (Acts 17). To Athenians who knew Greek literature and questioned him about his preachings, St. Paul quoted Greek poets. The aim, then, is to find a common level of understanding with the hearers of the word. Only at first glance might it appear that Paul puts faith and reason in opposition (cf. 1 Cor. 1:18 ff.). In reality, he very often uses arguments from reason.[2] And he aims to make himself understood. He maintains that in the presence of the community he would rather speak a mere five words of understanding "than ten thousand words in an unknown tongue" (1 Cor. 14:19). In many passages, he expresses concern that the believers may be or may become or remain reasonable.[3]

So apologia is a means of keeping the Christian belief in touch with reason. Otherwise, belief has no connection with the world. The point is not that God must be defended against all reason, nor against anyone or anything. But faith must be defended, and it must be proved defensible within the forum of reason (not against reason). In this way, reason can catch up with faith. *Fides quaerens intellectum*—this is the well-known formula of Anselm of Canterbury, expressing that reason is an intrinsic part of belief, and theologia is a necessary requisite of faith. Human nature seeks an understanding of what it believes. The relationship thus sketched between faith and reason prevailed from the beginning of Christian theology to the end of the Middle Ages.

The Emergence of New Perspectives

Roughly from the beginning of the Renaissance, a new mode of viewing and of thinking arose. It is the time of the discovery of perspective. This is true for drawing, painting, and for thinking as well, because humans cannot but encounter reality by means of their senses, regardless of whether they encounter reality in a sensuous or spiritual way. In a letter, Petrarch described his great adventure of climbing Mont Ventoux near Avignon. What he pointed out was nothing less than the discovery of the landscape.[4] The adhesion of human beings to heaven and earth, which was still an unquestioned and accepted connection, without distance and perspective, broke in that moment, when a part of nature was cut out of the whole space by his personal sight; and, thus, he shaped a piece of land into a landscape. At the same time, the all-embracing cohesion in painting, caused previously by those golden backgrounds, was replaced by a perspectival view: things were depicted in distance to the viewer and as cut out of a whole and related to a personal sight.

Often, people presume that perspective means a relation of things to an eyepoint, or a pyramid of seeing with its peak in one's eye. According to Leonardo da Vinci, however, we have to think of *two* pyramids, one of which has its base at the horizon and its a peak in the eye of the spectator. The second, in contrast, has the basis in the human eye and its peak somewhere out at the horizon. The first pyramid offers only the material which is to be shaped by the second. Historians of art, however, have remarked that the paintings by Leonardo and his successors were almost never constructed in complete perspective. There is no equilibrium between the viewer's eye and the objects out there, and thereby pictures come to life. Anyhow, there are two pyramids, and both are in tension. It is a tension between the exterior and the interior world.

Since Leonardo's time, occidental thinking in general must be characterized as perspectival. This means that a human being no longer is simply a part of the world and no longer perceives the structure of the world by "enduring" it. Leonardo's theory marks the end of "unconscious participation," to use Descartes' term. *"Participation inconsciente"* means nonreflective and nonconceptual participation in contrast to *"relation consciente,"* which is a reflective-conscious thinking, opposing and relating things to itself. Now a distance has been created between the things of the exterior world and human consciousness, which has become only the material for the "world" which must be depicted and shaped by a human mind (cf. the second pyramid).

Perspective that had its base in the eye of the spectator grew more and more important. This can clearly be demonstrated with the principles of Cartesian philosophy.[5] René Descartes shows himself not content simply to perceive things at hand; according to him, the presence of phenomena alone is insufficient. He distinguishes logical relations and by them construes a structural order, by which the truth of things should become evident. Even more, truth itself has come to mean the relationship within a mental system. To find out the consistency of the structures of the world with supreme mental principles means, according to him, to comprehend with certainty. *Certitude* becomes a decisive category for this new mode of perspective thinking. And only a thinking that brings forth certainty in the knowledge of truth is called rational. Things which do not fit to a thought order are finally confined to the immense realm of the irrational. Perspective thinking, however, is always endangered, because the thinker has to create the basis of the pyramid quite by himself, like a demiurge; and he does so without being able to realize whether the base itself is or will be valid.

The Religious Impact of Uncertainty

What does the preceding account mean for religious thinking? No longer does reason endeavor to catch up with faith. Instead, belief has to justify itself before rational thinking under conditions imposed by rationality. Apologia now feels compelled to prove the possibility of revelation. This means that revelation has to be examined to see if it fits a thought system. Then, one has to gain certainty about whether revelation is indeed a fact. And as certitude is difficult to achieve, uncertainty and doubt prevail. They characterize the centuries since the Renaissance in a fourfold way: There are doubts about God's mercifulness, about his justice and his omnipotence, about knowledge of God, and lastly doubts about certitude itself.[6]

The first stage of uncertainty has been marked by Luther's quest to ascertain whether he could find a merciful God. He did not only ask for the truth of salvation in general. He yearned for certainty that he himself would be rescued; or, in his own words, he demanded "certitude of belief." He was not only concerned with the certitude of true knowledge, but also with the certainty of salvation through the knowledge of God. If such knowledge is worth its name, it must guarantee salvation, as Luther put it in his disputation at Heidelberg in 1518. And as to the natural knowledge of God derived from creation, he maintains, without denying its content of truth, that it is not in itself sufficient for or useful to anybody ("*nulli iam satis sit ac prosit*").[7]

Remember Luther's internal fight in the monastery. Its result could, in his opinion, only be either despair or absolute security. His difficulties arose from the fact that he related his own life situation to an image of God inherited from Ockhamism, in which God was seen as a far distant, sovereign, and almost arbitrary being. Therein we find elements of perspective thinking as shown above, though it may be true that Martin Luther, as often has been remarked, was one of the last medieval men. But medieval life was naturally embedded in a firm structural order that gave an unquestionable security: the Church with its means of grace and salvation. One lived, if you like, in "*participation inconsciente*," whereas Luther shows elements of *"relation consciente."* He felt compelled to strive very consciously for security. This impulse, however, is only one moment on the way to the discovery of the justifying God.

The second kind of quest for certainty has a typically modern shape. Of course, you do find the question of God's justice already in the Bible, for example, in Job and Psalm 73 and in many other passages; it is at least as old as the question of God's mercy. However, the question of God's justice did not become a main subject of concern, nor did it become an impulse to theological destruction, fraught with grave consequences, until the Renaissance. At issue is whether there is meaningful guidance for the course of the world and, in the end, whether God exists at all. Doubts about his mightiness are but the other side of the same coin. A God unable to rule over the course of the world appears to be a contradiction. If blind chance is the ruler, the world could no longer be seen as any one being's creation.

These kinds of doubt can also be found in Greek antiquity. In the drama of Heracles by Euripides, the hero, who had been punished with madness, had killed his children. In a telling moment he put the question: Did my madness not come from a God—where else did it come from? If it comes from a God, was he a God?—Here we see a transition from doubts about a divine domination to doubts of the quality of God and thereby of God's existence. To Euripides, the Gods have become questionable.

In the eighteenth century, however, the question of whether God is just or almighty became more radical. The earthquake of Lisbon, where thirty thousand or even sixty thousand people were killed, also stirred the religious world. In relation to former times, the difference of the question is not only a matter of quantity; the change is essential. When, for instance, the psalmist quarreled with God about his ruling, the divine reality remained untouched. And if God's traces cannot be found and his being is veiled, this is a sign of his majesty, as when the psalmist says: "Thy way is in the sea, and thy path in the great water, and thy footsteps are not known" (Ps. 77:19). One has to pay attention to the way the complaint had been uttered that God's footsteps—the evidence of his rule—cannot have been known. It is the way of prayer. The psalmist did not doubt the existence of God, and he took into account that God would hear his quarrel as well. Here we have a doubt *within* the framework of belief in God. With the end of the Middle Ages, however, an important shift took place.

The German Lutheran theologian Helmut Thielicke put it this way: "By identifying God with an autonomously moulded idea of justice—without asking Him any more who he is and what He wants to be taken for 'His' justice—by taking our selfmade yardsticks as our criterion of God's image, He who has thus been integrated into our scale of values becomes himself questionable. At the end of this story of doubts, belief in God is replaced by fatalism."[8] In these words, we have a pretty clear description of what we above called perspective thinking: things are related to a thought system (to the base of the second pyramid in the mind of the spectator). In this perspective, the typically modern mode of doubt about God's justice or power comes into being. It is no accident that now the term "theodicy" was coined (as in the title of a book by Leibniz in 1710). Theodicy means the justification and defense of God that are deemed necessary because of the gap between the evil realized in the world and the human idea of what divine justice or power should be. This is the place for defense of God in a proper sense.

Defense of God, in the eighteenth and nineteenth centuries, however, does not simply mean a pleading for faith against the impact of a rationality that is opposed to Christian belief. It is not true that persons of high rationality in this period were unwilling to believe, as if faith were of minor quality or lesser status than rationality. They do not deny faith. But they put the question: On what are the unquestioned values and views especially those which go back to Christian origins, legitimately *grounded*? One asks for the *"ratio rerum,"* the reason and foundation of all that is valid. And so the quest for certainty reaches its summit. Gotthold Ephraim Lessing, therefore, opposes the "law of inertia" of tradition. He asserts that it is unacceptable to believe just on the basis of authority. In 1749, when he was twenty, he wrote to his father that Christianity could not be taken over from parents just on trust. And Reimarus and Semler put questions such as: What is the justification for belief in a transcendent God who has revealed himself by the birth of his son and by that son's death and resurrection? Are there watertight *historical* arguments for it? Or are there *logical* reasons that make it credible, or other generally accepted standards which make it possible to believe in "facts" that have no parallel in history?

This skeptical attitude, occurring in many variations, demands a rejection of the claimed inheritance of truths. On certain conditions, however, it seems possible to stay with old truths; namely, if they can be accepted by insight and choice. In other words, when transmitted stories or values can be related to my standards of acceptance, then they are certain, autonomous, and credible. But what are my standards of acceptance? Are they themselves secure? Or do they depend on something else which simply remains unquestioned? It is thus obvious that in the periods to come, perspective thinking and the quest for certainty must pass through a crisis.

The kind of doubting that characterizes the nineteenth and twentieth centuries led to resignation concerning the knowledge of "last" truths, such as the ground, aim, and meaning of life, that is, truths that wear the stamp of religion. The only meaningful "religious" statement seems to be Pilate's question: "What is truth?" (John 18:38). It appears to many nowadays that it is impossible to have any security because we lack a certain ground and foundation (a "base" for the pyramid mentioned above). For many people the bases of our "truths" are shaped by interests and, therefore, are ideologies. Thus, truth never appears to be timeless; instead, it is a function of other realities for a time. Ideologies are temporary because they depend on social and economic realities and interests and change with them. Doubts do not refer to questions of truth any more, but only to the question of whether a certain ideology— and a religious statement as interpreted this way, too,—is adequate to given social and economic conditions and the corresponding consciousness. Any accusation of untruth obviously becomes meaningless! Charges now run thus: You are not with the times . . .; your ideology is obsolete. . . . In this context, a defense of the belief in God becomes impossible.

A Deeper Crisis

The crisis of perspective thinking, however, is even deeper than outlined above. The infectious germs already existed in the very beginning of this thinking. I already mentioned that since the Renaissance, people have no longer been content with the world at hand; the world was only meaningful when it became material for the world as shaped by the human mind. This was not only an interior process of thinking. The idea that a person is demiurge, or creator, gave impetus to the modern sciences. The rise of modern natural sciences would not have happened without perspective thinking. The scientist does not simply listen to reality and watch natural processes, he rather urges nature to give answers which are *relevant to a system created by the human mind*. Science, thus, reveals itself as a means of dominion over creation. In accordance with this, the outcome of modern sciences—technology—not only has the aim of being helpful or useful to humankind, it also achieves dominion over nature—and over man as well. Roughly since the Renaissance, people have ruled over and changed the world according to their own ideas. To know a thing, according to Thomas Hobbes, means "to imagine what we can do with it when we have it."[9]

In the long run, human persons, esteeming themselves creators, lost responsibility to the Maker of earth and heaven. Used to the attitude of methodological atheism, a mode of investigation *"esti deus no daretur,"* the scientist lost sight of what function God could have within the scientific system. He came to presume that humanity is only responsible to itself.

The result of that presumption is the world we live in. Of course, no judicious being would deny that natural sciences and technology have benefitted our lives immensely. The seamy side of this, however, has now dawned upon us. Our present condition is highlighted by catchwords such as exhausted energy supply; dangers from nuclear wastes; diminishing metal resources; endangered biosphere through the pollution of air, rivers, seas, and soil; exploitation of ground water reserves, etc. Many contemporary scientists have now become sensitive about this situation and, as will be shown in the next section, Christendom has increasingly come under attack, specifically because of its belief in the Creator-God.

"And Have Dominion . . .": God the Creator on Trial

The American historian Lynn White maintained in 1967 that the Judeo-Christian belief in the command of dominion— "Replenish the earth, and subdue it; and have dominion over the fish of the sea, and over the fowl of the air, and over every living thing that moveth upon earth" (Gen. 1:18b)—has brought forth an attitude of arrogance against nature.[10] He was not the first to assert this, but his contention apparently was fairly effective. He claims that the idea of human supremacy over nature, which suggests some dualism between human beings and nature as well as a relatedness of the creation to the humanity whom it must serve, resulted from this interpretation of the divine instruction of *dominium terrae*. This idea, according to White, gained influence between the ninth and thirteenth centuries and shaped the beginnings of modern technology, which went on to become exploitative. The results now threaten to fly out of control. If this happens, a lot of guilt would rest on Christianity.

White's charge is accepted by many authors. Can it be refuted? Surely not by the hint that one can find demolition of the environment also in cultures other than ours. And not only by ascertaining that in the Bible there are also elements of a preservative attitude, or that the biblical instruction to take command need not or even should not be interpreted in the sense of exploitation. It is rather a question of how Christianity understood this instruction during the course of its history, and what the actual effects were. White's thesis can only be proven false by historical investigations. A lot of work has been done on this issue.[11] We do not have space to report the results; it must suffice to indicate that only when the command of dominion had been detached from the Judeo-Christian context did it become associated with technical intervention. Our relation to nature became exploitative when nature was considered only under the aspect of utilization.

The early church fathers before St. Augustine realized that, according to Gen. 1:28, animals were not originally given to humankind for nourishment. Only after the Deluge, when the granting of dominion was repeated (Gen. 9), were they given for nutrition. Before the fall, a human being had only to arrange life with the animals—as a king and not as a despot. Being made in the image of God, a human person was bound and related to God; he or she was to act only in his name, as his representative on earth. The order to subdue the earth was understood as an instruction for agriculture. Some church fathers even asserted that after the fall the command to subdue the earth was rescinded forever. Others tried to align the idea of *dominium terrae* with pre-Christian philosophy, especially with the Stoics. It was in this kind of philosophy that for the first time the idea of anthropocentrism and even of humanity's ontological superiority was developed. The understanding of nature in the Stoa, however, was static: Nature was essentially completed; its development or fulfillment by humankind, was thus unthinkable. Origen interpreted the dominion over the earth as a restriction against human intervention in the course of nature. Early Benedictine monks understood their work as cooperation with God in an eschatological sense. Their gardens, therefore, had the shape of an imaginative paradise. Work in an eschatological context has to be joyful; mechanical tools, thus, were soon invented to do unpleasant jobs. In this atmosphere, some technology developed already in the twelfth and thirteenth centuries.

After intermediate stages, the Renaissance brought a great shift. Mechanical technology became part of humanity's ability to create something new. Dominion over the earth was no longer seen as founded in the fact that humanity is the image of God. Leonardo da Vinci proclaimed: "O investigator of things! Do not boast of the knowledge of things brought forth by nature in its usual course; rather delight in knowing the aim and purpose of things designed by this [the human] spirit!"[12]

Francis Bacon, finally, declared that the goals God has put into things are unknowable. Not knowing the inner tendencies of nature, persons are in their actions independent from the Creator. Even if we had knowledge of what things themselves are aiming at, this would not only be useless, it could prevent us from improving nature and utilizing it. Therefore, Bacon rejects teleological thinking. The investigation of the *causae finales* is, according to one of his well-known sayings, like a virgin dedicated to God who does not give birth to anything.[13] By causal-mechanical twisting, nature reveals itself more than by its natural tendencies. Human beings in this way regain the dominion over the world they had lost in the fall, as Bacon believed along with some of those church fathers to whom I referred. Humanity now thought itself capable of returning nature to its ideal condition in paradise—independently of God.

Commitments to goals beyond human needs and interests faded out in the last century, and the combination of causal-mechanical sciences with technology brought about the exploitation of nature. Whereas a certain two-dimensionality of the Christian relationship to nature—according to Gen. 2:15, God put human life "into the garden of Eden to dress and to keep it"—was maintained even in the Age of Enlightenment, this two-dimensionality of anthropocentrism and preservation of nature got lost in the Industrial Revolution. The development that was now introduced led to the exploitation of nature.

To sum up: The exploitation of nature that rapidly resulted after the Industrial Revolution was not caused by the Judeo-Christian belief in the Creator and his command to dominate the earth. It commenced when the idea of dominion got separated from its Christian context. Though the idea that humanity is called to complete the creation of God has deep roots in the history of

Christian belief, it only became menacing when people tried to shape the world according to their own imagination alone and, without exception, to their own wants; in other words, when they perspectively related nature to a thought system created by the human mind.

The Perspectives We Need

The reason for our present condition is linked to the outcome of perspective thinking, as I indicated above, since this kind of thinking means distance to the exterior world and "objectivity." Especially as more and more emphasis has been put on the perspective based in the human mind (i.e. in the sense of the second pyramid), the world has become a *mere* object, an object for scientific utilization and technological exploitation. On the other hand, the perspective that is based in the world (i.e., in the sense of the first pyramid) has been neglected, so that man has lost his capacity to see the world as "subject," too.

What can we do now? Of course, it is impossible to turn back to a pre-perspective society, when people belonged in unquestioned unity with God, nature, and humanity. All our scientific and technological achievements, and our sociological structures as well, would be so radically called into question that such a model would seem a romantic Utopia that nobody could seriously hope to achieve. As we have seen, it was not, properly speaking, perspective thinking that caused our dilemma, but the one-sided stress on the perspective based in the human mind. We cannot but continue to affirm perspective thinking. But we now have to emphasize the perspective which earth presents to us, too, instead of seeing earth merely as a means for production and reorganization. We have to train our capacity for *per*ception and *re*ception. Perhaps reception must prevail over doing.

To clarify what I just said, we should look at scientific language and models of thinking. The perspective that has its base in the human mind can be related to a mode of scientific thinking that is called causal-mechanistic. Asking for the cause of something means, according to the generally accepted Hempel-Oppenheim scheme, to ask for antecedent and accompanying conditions, and for natural laws by which these conditions bring forth an occurrence that has to be explained. In other words, we relate observed "facts" with mental structural systems. Of course, there are no "objectively"

observed facts, because observation implies the isolation of a consequence "B" caused by the conditions "A" within an ongoing flux,
and this means highly mental activity on the part of the observing
subjects. All depends on where we focus the "peak of the pyramid."

Inversely, the perspective that has its base in nature and its peak in
our mind can be identified as a *teleological* perspective.[14] Within this
perspective occurs perception and understanding of tendencies in
nature. But understanding differs from explanation, as delineated
above.

Understanding does not stress how to produce a thing. It is no
wonder that the founders of modern natural sciences neglected or
rejected teleology. Nominalists already claimed that the goals of
nature are unrecognizable, that there is nothing in reality which
corresponds to the universal term *finis*. But the motive of the
Renaissance scientists was not as much an epistemological one as a
question of dominion over nature. Teleology cannot make it possible to predict events; nor can understanding of goals be achieved
other than *a posteriori*.

With the rejection of regional and particular teleology in physical
sciences, not much was lost—all the less, as great spirits of that age such
as Kepler, Newton, von Huygens, and Leibniz continued to
regard God as guarantor of the final destiny of the whole world.
Teleology, however, was completely ignored in the nineteenth century.
The theory of evolution seemed especially incompatible with the idea
of teleology. The question "why?" prevailed over "what for?"

Recent investigations, however, make clear that even the physical
terminology of Darwinism is permeated with teleological ideas.[15]
Surprisingly, there is even a rediscovery of teleology by natural
sciences nowadays. Teleology appears to be "necessary" in order to
make a distinction of rank in the means to an end.

For a long time, scientists have claimed that teleology is "unscien-
tific." Indeed, the question "what for?" does not properly speaking,
fit the horizon of scientific investigations. Natural sciences, however, owe their existence to the rise of perspective thinking; and
there always is an interconnection of *two* pyramids of viewing, as
indicated above. Surely, the pyramid based in the human mind
remains the only proper methodological context of natural sciences;
yet science has to hold itself open to the fact that this pyramid must
be completed by the second one.

The necessity for the teleological perspective became obvious in
the same measure as we became aware of our ecological dilemma.

Within the context of causal-mechanical explanation and dominion over the earth, one can at best put the question: How can I restrict my activities so as to exploit nature most beneficially without harming it? Restrictions do not mean an abolishment of scientific dominion over nature, which in principle expands infinitely. But this kind of expansiveness put in practice has revealed itself as incompatible with the finite world we live in. If the question of restriction remains anthropocentric, this might lead to giant catastrophes for humanity.

We must turn to nature itself. In our mind we have to represent things as they are themselves and to respect their selfhood. Selfhood is taken to mean not functioning *only* as a means to something else, but having a meaning in itself. It is the teleological perspective that reveals the goals things have in themselves. There is a hierarchy of goals. The lowly must serve the higher ranking. We have to use animals for our nourishment, but to respect their selfhood means the responsibility not to exterminate their species. Yet science as such is unable to give reasons for the preservation of all species: why should we preserve animals, after all, that are completely useless to us? Though the discussion of teleology is, especially in biology, rising again, the question of goals in themselves is not a proper scientific one. Philosophy and religion are called for.

The reduction of our knowledge of nature to its causal-mechanistic explanation since the Age of Renaissance has been led by a certain willfulness: the drive to achieve dominion over the earth. For this reason the teleological perspective faded out. People have purposes, and they try to subdue nature to achieve them. This is legitimate, of course. Even more, our existence in the world today depends on this procedure, but keeping the counterbalance of the teleological perspective is also important. What can physical sciences say about the goals things have in themselves? They can maintain that the goal of everything is self-preservation, but they are not able to explain the sense and value of self-preservation. What can one say, from a scientific viewpoint, to prevent somebody from plucking a rare and beautiful flower growing in a place usually inaccessible? Philosophy might provide some rationale that could prevent us from wantonly plucking the flower; then again it might not.

At this point religion, in the sense of belief in the Creator, enters the discussion. For the Judeo-Christian belief that our world is created by God has a strong teleological element, as is obvious in such biblical statements as: "For Him, and through Him, and to Him, are all things: to whom be glory for ever. Amen" (Rom. 11:36).[16] Does religious belief add a new goal outside of the things themselves, a goal beyond the selfhood? No! To say something exists in relation to God or for his glory does not mean that it is a means to a certain purpose. It rather means that such a thing is "more" ultimately an end in itself than if it would only exist for its own sake. As all things, according to Christian belief, find in God their origin and their impulse, they have in him their center of being and their own goal. Regarding a thing in its final relatedness to God implies that we do not esteem it merely as a means for our own use, but that we acknowledge its selfhood and affirm it *absolutely*. Belief in the Creator gives things absolute dignity in themselves. The Creator, thus, reveals himself as counsel for the defense of nature as a goal in itself.

The starting point of my essay was the statement that theology is essentially apologia for faith in God. Since the Renaissance, the defense of God has taken place in the general context of the quest for certainty. This means that all problems have been related to a thought system. In theodicy, for example, observed evils were put in relationship to what men thought God's justice or power ought to be. From there the question arose whether our self-made yardsticks for judgment were adequate. In this way, the defense of God has become nearly impossible.

Nevertheless, attacks on God have not ceased; in fact, new points for them have been formulated. In recent days, faith in the Creator-God has been cited as being the preeminent cause of our present ecological crisis. This argument is, as I have indicated, unconvincing. Quite the contrary! I have tried to demonstrate that belief in the Creator-God can provide a proper rationale for defending nature also for its own sake, so that nature will not be preserved only for enhancement of technical and economical utilization.

The tables have been turned; the "defended" Creator has become the defender of nature's goals. Even more, belief in the Creator has proved indispensable for supplying ultimate reasons for the preservation of nature. Sometimes it is said that God has never ceased talking to us, but that we lost our ability to hear God speaking. Sometimes people wake up when crisis hits. The ecological situation is crucial. Could it be that a new sensibility of the world as a creation is growing and that the defense of our environment will turn out to be an apologia for and also from the Creator-God?

NOTES

1. See G. Bornkamm, "Glaube und Vernunft bei Paulus," in G. Bornkamm, *Studien zu Antike und Urchristentum: Gesammelte Aufsätze* (Munich: Kaiser Verlag, 1963), 2:119–37.

2. Ibid., 122–28.

3. Ibid., 137.

4. See J. Gebser, *Ursprung und Gegenwart,* vol. 1, *Die Fundamente der aperspektivischen Welt* (Schaffhausen: Novalis, 1949), 25. See also H. Dolch, *Kausalität im Verständnis des Theologen und der Begründer neuzeitlicher Physik* (Freiburg: Herder, 1954), 33–40.

5. See H. Glockner, *Die europäische Philosophie von den Anfängen bis zur Gegenwart* (Stuttgart: Reclam-Verlag, 1954), 405–27.

6. See H. Thielicke, *Glauben und Denken in der Neuzeit: Die grossen Systeme der Theologie und Religionsphilosophie* (Tübingen: Mohr, 1983), 34–47.

7. M. Luther, "Die Heidelberger Disputation, 1518," in *Luther's, Werke in Auswahl,* ed. E. Vogelsang (Berlin: W. de Gruyter, 1963), 5:388.

8. Thielicke, 41.

9. Thomas Hobbes, *Leviathan,* in *English Works* (London: J. Bohn, 1839), 3:13.

10. L. White, "The Historical Roots of Our Ecologic Crisis," *Science* 155 (1967): 1203–7.

11. See, for example, U. Krolzik, "'Machet Euch die Erde untertan . . .!' und das christliche Arbeitsethos," in *Frieden mit der Natur,* ed. K. M. Meyer-Abich (Freiburg: Herder, 1979), 174–95.

12. Quoted from H. R. Müller-Schwefe, *Technik und Glaube: Eine permanente Herausforderung* (Göttingen-Mainz: Vandenhoeck & Ruprecht-Matthias Grünewald, 1971), 94.

13. Francis Bacon, "De dignitate et augmentis scientiarum," 3:5, in *The Works of Lord Bacon* (London, 1841), 2:340: "nam causarum finalium inquisitio sterilis est, et, tanquam virgo Deo consecrata, nihil parit."

14. Within this context, I do not make any distinction between "teleomatic," "teleonomy," and "teleology."

15. See R. Spämann and R. Loew, *Die Frage wozu?: Geschichte und Wiederentdeckung des teleologischen Denkens* (Munich: Pieper, 1981).

16. See also 1 Cor. 8:6, Eph. 1:10b, Col. 1:16, and Heb. 2:10.

9

Humanity, Being, and World History

EUGENE T. LONG

In his essay "The Defense of God," Frederick Sontag is issuing a challenge which stretches beyond the limits of traditional religious thought and institutions. He is calling on those who participate in religious ways of life to acknowledge their share of the responsibility for failing to achieve a social solidarity which goes beyond the limits of race, creed, and nationality. He is also calling for a reassessment of those religious ideas and institutions which the religious claim to be important for human fulfillment but which in many cases appear to have contributed more to human disarray than to human solidarity. His challenge to the religious is not unlike the challenge of some neo-Marxists to order Marxists to reevaluate their roots in light of the failure to realize the expected world brotherhood of workers.

In this essay, I want to select one question that comes to the surface at several places in Sontag's paper. I would put the question this way. If persons of different religious traditions could agree that they share in common something that might be called a religious attitude or way of life, and if they believe that this way of life is important to humanity and its search for social solidarity, then how can they proceed toward this goal without repeating those disputes which have often contributed more to social disarray than social solidarity? At the end of his paper, Sontag calls on the religious to unite, and to defend the divine traditions in every land. But how can this be done when, more often than not, our defenses result in misunderstanding at best and war at worst? It is difficult to counter the claim that religious ways of life have often contributed to suffering and disarray in human life, or that religious ways of life are merely examples of ideological commitments through which persons attempt to control others. Even some so-called ecumenical discussions often seem to be aimed more at bureaucratic control than genuine dialogue. We are stung by Nietzsche's criticism of religion as a way of seeking power over others just because it so often strikes home.

It is tempting perhaps to accept as inevitable the lack of social solidarity in the world and the religious contribution to it. After all, we are different and we no longer believe in most cases that social progress is inevitable. For the person, however, who is committed both to social solidarity and to a religious way of life, this may not be a live option. It may be that social progress is not inevitable, but we certainly do not know that it is impossible. To give up hope for a more human world may be in fact to give up something which is essential to our being fully human. In the absence of hope there would seem to be only despair and a kind of retreat from efforts to realize our fullest humanity in relation with others. Even if we could tolerate intellectual provincialism (and I doubt that we can without running the risk of irrational commitments), we cannot, it would seem, tolerate the suffering that occurs when people armed with their ideologies threaten to destroy others. Certainly, those who are victims cannot ignore this. How then can those who profess a religious way of life meet others who profess a different religious way of life when they both share the desire for social solidarity and human fulfillment?

We may take up attitudes of indifference towards each other. We may simply be content with our own tradition and ignore the claims of others. But this, as Karl Jaspers has said, may be the greatest form of intolerance. Most of us would prefer to be argued against than simply ignored. We might without reflection accept the view that all religions are after the same thing and propose a kind of passive tolerance of differences. But this kind of recognition of others is difficult to make consistent with the commitments we hold, and the belief that our commitments make and should make a difference in life. Perhaps we could attempt a syncretism of religions in which we make lists of what can be agreed to; but previous efforts at this appear to have failed, and, even if we could reach agreement, the result may be a watered down set of propositions far removed from the life of faith. Faith, after all, is not merely assent to some set of propositions. It has to do with attitudes and commitments that are believed to result in changes in our lives. If religious commitment is important, and if it is the case that in some sense we are historical beings, limited in our world views by the historicity of our own beings, we will have to avoid either taking refuge in mere dogmatic claims or thinking of our religious ways of life as ones in which commitments are not taken seriously.

I am assuming in this essay that our diverse religious ways of life include commitments which we take seriously, and that there are important differences in the ways in which we give expression to and justify these commitments. If this is the case, our discussions must get beyond the level of sentimentality and indifference. We must get to those root issues which have to do with how we live and think about our being in the world. Yet if we are also serious in our interest in social solidarity and if we believe that the religious way of life has something significant to offer toward achieving this end, we will have to get beyond the arrogance that has sometimes characterized such discussions.

My intent in this essay is a modest one. I want to propose an interpretive framework within which discussions might take place across religious and cultural lines in the interest of both the religious way of life and social solidarity. Many religious persons in meeting other religious persons have acknowledged something in common. It was Paul Tillich, I believe, who said after a world tour that he had seen examples of ultimate concern throughout the world religions. There appears to be some sense of transcendence or ultimacy that goes beyond the boundaries of our various historical religions. It may be, probably is, the case that we are Hindus, Christians, Jews, Buddhists, and so forth in part as a result of accidents of birth. That is, we have come to understand what it means to be human and to acknowledge the transcendent dimensions within human experience through those several traditions which happen to be a part of our history. What we share in common are not these various traditions but our humanity and our desire to come to understand more clearly who we are and who we can be. I do not mean to deny that conversions can take place or that there are legitimate and important differences for which we must argue. Nor do I mean to suggest that an adequate expression of what it means to be fully human can be found equally in all traditions. Even within the same tradition we will find important differences for which we must account and decide which is the more adequate. I do want to suggest, however, that in our efforts to understand what it is to be fully human, each of us brings a particular, inherited history, and this sets limits to efforts to give a final account of the being of human existence.

Perhaps all religions share an attitude in common which points us toward an understanding of what is ultimate or transcendent in human experience.[1] But how we give expression to this transcendent dimension of human experience will depend initially at least on the traditions and categories which we have inherited. Having said this, one can also say, I believe, that there is a sense in which the world at which one religious person looks and the world at which other religious persons and secularists look is the same. For example, Christian theologians may speak out of the experiences of a particular historical tradition, but it would seem that they share in common with all persons human experience within which the particular historical revelations of the Christian community have to be received and comprehended. And just because of this they cannot hide behind a set of propositions about humanity and God which they inherit and assert in competition with other ideologies. If they are to communicate with others, they will have to make that human experience clear in relation to which they understand the Christian revelation. The emphases on transcendence, otherness, nothingness and so on which we encounter in all religions would seem to suggest that the religious way of life cannot be understood adequately as just one ideology set over against others. The Scottish theologian Ronald Gregor Smith puts this in a pointed way in the context of the Christian tradition when he argues that in Jesus' cry of dereliction from the cross, the world is believed to be cleared of all Gods, of all ideologies, powers, and hopes. The assurances which humankind seeks to build up within the world in order to give certainty to its life are put to an end.[2]

I do not mean by this to suggest that the religious way of life is removed from the world and set over against it. On the contrary, I would argue that it is precisely in the midst of our efforts to understand and realize our possibilities as beings in the world that the religious way of life can come to be understood and appropriated. The problem is not that we emphasize too much the human and not enough the divine. The problem is that we, including religious persons, do not emphasize enough the human. What we share across our various cultural boundaries is our humanity, and it is just here that we can find our common ground. On these grounds, it seems to me, Christians, Jews, Hindus, secularists, and others stand side by side. What we share is an interest in what we are as human beings and what we can be. The important question here has to do with how we can achieve our fullest humanity.

Ultimately, of course, Christian believers look beyond themselves to the grace of God for the fulfillment of their being; but if, as Christianity claims, we are creatures of God and in some way dependent on God for fulfillment, this should show itself in the exploration of what it means to be fully human. To put this another way, the Christian theologian should be able to locate God on the ontological map of the being of human existence. And, if other religious traditions are able to place their ultimate categories on the ontological map of human existence, we should be in a better position to understand how the categories are being used to discuss whether or not some categories make more sense of human experience of existence and being than others.

What I am proposing as a beginning place for genuine discussions across cultural lines is what some philosophers would call a phenomenology of existence and being, and some theologians would call a natural theology. The intent is not to prove God's existence as was the case in much traditional Western natural theology. The intent is to show where on the map of human existence the various religious categories find their place. It may be, probably is, the case that such descriptions or interpretations of existence and being can never be completely free of the cultural traditions that we bring with us. Our efforts to understand our experience of ourselves in the world take place within some framework, some point of view which helps make us what we are. But perhaps we can distinguish between what Ninian Smart calls a highly ramified and a relatively unramified approach to such interpretations. That is, we can seek to avoid imposing a preconceived interpretative scheme on our analysis of what it means to be human. In so doing we may be able to identify those characteristics of humanity which appear to transcend the limits of our particular cultures and traditions. Just as, for example, we can discover in the work of such Western philosophers as Karl Jaspers and Martin Heidegger a notion similar to the Christian notion of grace which is understood to be essential to the realization of a full humanity, so we may expect to find something similar in non-Christian religious traditions even though they do not carry the particular theological beliefs associated with Christianity.

The task that is being proposed here is not one that can be carried out in a brief essay. It would entail a full description and interpretation of the human experience of existence and being. I can only point to certain Western philosophers such as Heidegger and Jaspers and certain Christian thinkers such as Donald Evans and John

Macquarrie who are engaged in this task. Keiji Nishitani seems to me to be proceeding in a related manner from an Eastern point of view.[3] For my purposes here, I have to be satisfied with merely calling attention to what these persons are doing. This much, however, should be said. The task that I am proposing would have to be both a descriptive and a normative one. That is, we would have to focus not only on those possible ways of being which make up what we call human being, we would also have to focus on what we consider to be the most human way of existing, and on what attitudes are essential to the realization of the most human way of being.

In such an undertaking we would discover, I suspect, that in all traditions there is a recognition of what might be called a committed versus a noncommitted view of life. A retreat from commitment would seem to result in a floating mode of existence, a life without direction, whereas commitment suggests a unified form of life, a life with direction. And in exploring this committed form of life we might also discover that the various religious traditions all point in some way beyond the merely empirical to transcendent dimensions in human experience, and ultimately to a kind of basic confidence or trust in reality. If this were the case, we would then be in a position to discuss the various descriptions of reality to see in what sense they are adequate to the experience of commitment in life. It may be just here that we would find a fundamental difference between religious and nonreligious ways of life. That is, religious persons spelling out what they consider to be fundamental to the fulfillment of human existence may in various ways give expression to a basic trust or confidence in reality, and claim to discover in reality a meaning or direction for human existence already given. This attitude of basic or cosmic trust, what Macquarrie calls trust in the wider range of being, has been identified by many Christian theologians from Luther onwards as an essential ingredient of religious faith. Christian theologians would identify the ground of this ultimate trust as God, but there would seem to be no reason to expect to find this attitude of ultimate trust or confidence only in Western theistic traditions. One might expect to find similar discussions wherever one finds discussions of what it means to be fully human. The difference would probably be in how we identify the ground of that trust. This opens up the possibility for genuine discussions concerning which categories make the most sense of this commitment. At least it might allow us to discover that religious persons share something like this trust in common with many, including perhaps some nonreligious persons. There are cases, for example, in which persons professing no religious attitude seem to acknowledge something like what we have been calling cosmic or basic trust. In such cases our question would be whether we can make sense of such an attitude in the absence of some kind of religious interpretation.

To have faith is to have some kind of commitment, something that gives direction to one's life. Thus I may have faith in my friend, or in my wife and children, or in my chosen vocation. Without such commitments I tend to drift from one moment to the next; I become a kind of dilettante. Faith or commitment would seem in some sense to be essential to human fulfillment. Without it there would be no focus or direction to life. For the religious person, however, faith or commitment ultimately points beyond what can be specified empirically to a transcendent ground which gives confidence that somehow things are all right. Faith in this sense is what I would call an existential attitude, a believing in something or someone and, if I am religious, ultimately in reality itself as supportive of the human condition.

It is important, particularly in cross cultural discussion, to keep in mind the distinction between faith as an existential attitude and belief through which I give cognitive content to this attitude. Wilfred Cantwell Smith is correct, I believe, to point out that until the modern era, biblical faith had more to do with loyalty, commitment and trust than it did with assenting to a series of propositions. Faith, not belief, he argues, is the central biblical category, and statements which arise from faith are in some sense personal statements, statements made about man and his relations to the world and transcendence. That the modern era talks so much about religious belief rather than faith is the result of a turn which has taken place in our uses of "faith" and "belief." This is indicative of a turn in the world view of Western culture, a turn which has been aided and abetted by theologians. In the modern era, faith has tended to converge with belief, and the latter has shifted in meaning from the personal to the impersonal and the true to the dubious. This has resulted in a shift from the view in which believing in God meant trusting and responding to transcendent qualities in one's environment, to assenting to a set of dubious or problematic propositions.[4]

Smith is, of course, not the only person to call attention to this distinction between faith and belief. Indeed, in contemporary thought some have so emphasized faith over against belief that there are grounds for fearing that faith is bereft of any intellectual content. Nevertheless there is an important point here, and I have chosen to refer to Smith just because he is a historian of world religions who is now attempting to tackle some of the normative issue which arise when religious persons meet each other across cultural lines. If I believe in or have faith in someone, there are implicit, at least, certain beliefs about that person. Just because of this, faith can never be totally separated from belief. If, however, this distinction is forgotten and faith is identified with belief, then discussions among religions tend to reduce to competing ideologies.

If there is a common ground among world religions, it is likely to be found at the level of faith as basic trust understood as an essential ingredient of what it means to be human; and if we recognize that our different beliefs represent efforts to give expression to the implications of this faith, we are less likely to approach such discussions with totalitarian and exclusivistic attitudes. We may expect to discover in the dialogue between religions that in some cases we will need to revise our beliefs as we make an effort to give fuller expression to our faith. A certain tenacity is no doubt required with regard to our beliefs. If they are central to the committed life that we lead, it is unlikely that we will give them up whenever we encounter opposition. At the same time, we need to recognize that our beliefs represent our efforts to give the most adequate account of our faith, and, unless we are fanatics, we should recognize the possibility that these beliefs will need revision as we go about the effort of further clarifying and understanding our commitments.

I have suggested above that faith as basic trust or confidence in reality issues in Christian thought in a commitment to God as the source and ground of this confidence and trust. As such, God may be understood as the source and goal of humanity in its search for fulfillment. If one thinks of God in this way, I do not believe that we can consistently understand God to be an absolute monarch or tyrant who directs us contrary to our resolve to fulfill our potentiality. On the contrary, it would seem that God would have to be related to us analogously to the way in which Heidegger suggests that we are authentically related to others. The authentic relation to others is one in which we enable others to realize their fullest possibilities. It is a standing in ahead of the other, a drawing him toward his humanity as opposed to standing in for him and taking over responsibility for his being. By analogy it would seem that if we are to make our idea of

God consistent with our search for and realization of our highest possibilities, God could not be understood to contradict our search for fulfillment and our confidence that reality is trustworthy. Instead of standing in for us, taking our place so to speak, God would have to be a God who lets be, who enables us to realize our possibilities, who draws us toward our fullest humanity. God, it would seem, would have to be somewhat like the God described by Charles Hartshorne: "the unsurpassable inspiring genius of all freedom, not the all determining coercive tyrant."[5]

If God is understood in this way then perhaps we can see a way forward toward a full realization of what it means to be human and a unity with those persons who seek fulfillment of their humanity. Freedom would seem to be a root concept in all of our talk about realizing our fullest humanity and any action on our part which would seek to stand in for or take away the freedom of others to realize their humanity would be tyrannical, an action that could be defended only by a tyrannical God. God does not defend himself perhaps just because he is not tyrannical. To be coercive would be to destroy the very ingredient which is central to realizing our humanity. But if it is the nature of reality to let us be, to enable us to realize our fullest humanity in conformity with reality, our relations with others ought to be one of enabling others to realize their being. If God is an inspiring genius of freedom and not a tyrant, then why should he be tyrannical in relating with others? Does not such action contradict our search for humanity and our basic trust in reality? Freedom is not, of course, without its constraints, but where there is freedom it would seem there is hope, hope perhaps that man can cooperate toward the goal of the achievement of our fullest humanity. For in Christianity this ultimately means hope for the realization of our being as creatures of God. To the extent that we cooperate with God's inspiring genius of freedom, we may be said to be acting in defense of God. To the extent that we contradict this direction and stand over against others armed with our religious ideologies, we oppose that very reality in which we put our trust and confidence.

Thus far it has been suggested that faith appears on the map of human existence as basic trust or confidence in reality, that for Christians at least the ground of that confidence is called God and that God should be thought in a manner consistent with our search for the fulfillment of human existence. In this context it was suggested that God might be thought of as inspiring genius of freedom rather than powerful tyrant. It is, of course, with reference to the ultimate or transcendent dimensions of human experience that we encounter our most obvious difficulties in meeting the religious ways of life across cultural lines. Indeed, even within one tradition such as Christianity one encounters many characteristics of ultimate reality, some of which seem to be in conflict and some of which may represent different poles of the same experience of ultimate reality. When we cross cultural traditions, however, we run into conflicts of an even more radical kind. There are, we might say, many images or faces of God. This should not surprise us. These various images may be taken as imperfect efforts to give symbolic expression to that which is at the foundation of our basic trust and confidence in reality. It is to be expected that one would bring the best of one's own heritage and tradition to bear on such an important subject. From a Christian point of view, if God is an inspiring genius of freedom we should expect God to inspire us to choose our authentic way of being through those vehicles which help make us what we are. For the same reason, we should not expect that God would disclose himself in a definitive way in only one place and time. Only a tyrannical God would engage in such activity.

If we could agree to this we would be in a position, I believe, to understand how one can be committed to and come to understand one's being in the world in the context of one's history and tradition while remaining open and receptive to the possibility that our efforts to give expression to humanity and reality may be deepened or perhaps even altered in conversation with others. Can we go further than this? Can we actually confront the conflicting ways in which various religions speak of the ultimate or transcendent? What do we do, for example, when our view of God as inspiring genius of freedom appears to conflict with Islam, in which the emphasis is on God's sovereignty and power? Or what do we do when our view of the ultimate as transcendent is brought up against Hinayana Buddhism, in which the ultimate appears to be an immanent cosmic order?

To this question I have no clear answer, but perhaps this much can be said. It appears to me, to paraphrase Paul Tillich, that humans cannot be ultimately concerned about anything that is less than the fully human. If this is the case, then we should expect to find reflected in our interpretations of the ultimate those various dimensions of human experience which make up what it is to be human. Here we confront conflicting tendencies. We think of ourselves as in some sense immanent to the material world, in some sense bound by it; yet we also think that in some sense we transcend it, control it, and use it for our purposes. We also think of ourselves as free, as having a future; yet this freedom is understood to take place within certain constraints, within the context of what we are and have been. We are in some sense individuals, unique, unlike any other; yet we are also social beings. What we are and what we can be has to do with our relations with others. We are at times loving beings, and we want the other to be the best that he or she can be. But with this love at times comes judgment, a calling of persons to realize that they have fallen away from their highest potentialities. At times this can lead us to take over the other person; we can smother that person, or substitute our being for his or hers. There are many such tensions within human existence as we seek to become what we can be within the context of what we are and have been.

When, from the perspectives of what it means to be human, we then by analogy talk about the ultimate ground of humanity, the ground of our basic trust and understanding of ourselves, it is to be expected that we will at times emphasize such categories as transcendence, judgment, power, and self-identity, and at other times immanence, freedom, becoming, and loving. This can help us to understand why within the Christian tradition, for example, we find different examples in talk of God. And perhaps it is this which also accounts for some of the differences between religions and between their conceptions of ultimate reality. If in Islam, for example, the emphasis is on the power of God, there is also mention of mercy; and if in Buddhism the emphasis is on immanence, there is also talk of transcendence.

These various polarities in our descriptions of ultimate reality suggest a need for engaging in discussions within our own traditions and with other traditions to see to what extent these differences are contradictory, to what extent they can be reconciled, or at least to what extent they may be understood to be giving expression to various dimensions of the experience of the ground of our basic trust. To engage in such a task would be in some sense to move beyond the limits of our particular historical traditions, to seek a more universal or essentialy self-interpreting discourse about ultimate reality, to engage in metaphysical or ontological inquiry.

This suggestion itself may seem to put another stumbling block in the way of East-West discussion, because in the East religion and philosophy are not as distinct as they often are in the West. Philosophy, like religion, in the East often has to do with the search for salvation. If, however, we think of metaphysics or ontology in the sense that followers of Heidegger and Jaspers do, this difference may not be as great as initially thought. For them the question of the meaning of human existence and the question of being are closely connected. Indeed, some Westerners who no longer identify themselves with a particular religious tradition look to Jaspers or Heidegger as providing a kind of substitute for institutional religion, a kind of natural religion.

The approach to metaphysics which is being suggested here would continue to give primacy to the human experience of existence and being. It would continue to focus on our quest for our fullest humanity, but it would look to an interpretive scheme or metaphysics as part of the process of understanding, explaining, and justifying the religious commitments which arise out of this quest. It is probably the case that we will discover no one interpretive scheme which is fully adequate to our interpretations of human experience. This may not be possible even within the context of our own traditions and is even more problematic when our context is humankind in world history. But we may discover that our efforts will at many points overlap and complement each other, in which case we may be in a position to say that the symbols regarding ultimate reality which we find in one historical tradition may be pointing to an interpretation of reality similar to what we find in other traditions. In some cases, of course, we may be convinced that some schemes or concepts contradict each other and it would be unreasonable to hold to both. Here, I believe, it is incumbent upon us to try and decide which is the more adequate. It is interesting in this regard to note that there is evidence of a fundamental shift in the way that contemporary Western philosophers and theologians understand God and God's relation to the world. There appears to be something of a consensus among many which points to a more immanental God, and a more organic understanding of the relation between God and world. In this regard perhaps Western thought today stands much closer to Eastern thought than in the days when classical theistic views dominated Western discussions of religion.

NOTES

1. It would be interesting in this regard to consider Karl Jaspers's empirical claim that there is an axial period in history around 500 B.C. in which the world religions by which human beings still live were created. "What is new about this age, in all three areas of the world, is that man becomes conscious of Being as a whole, of himself and his limitations. . . . He experiences absoluteness in the depths of selfhood and in the lucidity of transcendence. . . . These paths are widely divergent in their convictions and dogma, but common to all of them is man's reaching out beyond himself by growing aware of himself within the whole of Being and the fact that he can tread them only as an individual on his own. . . . Revelation is the form taken by particular historical creeds, experience is accessible to man as man. We—all men—can share the knowledge of the reality of this universal transformation of mankind during the Axial Period." *The Origin and Goal of History* (London: Routledge and Kegan Paul, 1953), 2–19.

2. See my discussion of this in *God, Secularization and History: Essays in Memory of Ronald Gregor Smith,* ed. Eugene Thomas Long (Columbia: University of South Carolina Press, 1974).

3. See Karl Jaspers, *Philosophy* (Chicago: University of Chicago Press, 1970); Martin Heidegger, *Being and Time* (New York: Harper and Row, 1962); Donald Evans, *Faith, Authenticity and Morality* (Toronto: University of Toronto Press, 1980); Keiji Nishitani, *Religion and Nothingness* (Berkeley: University of California Press, 1982). John Macquarrie, *In Search of Humanity* (London: SCM Press, 1982).

4. Wilfred Cantwell Smith, *Belief and History* (Charlottesville: University Press of Virginia, 1977).

5. Charles Hartshorne, "Divine Absoluteness and Divine Relativity," in *Transcendence,* ed. H. W. Richardson and D. R. Cutler (Boston: Beacon, 1969), 169. Cited in Macquarrrie, *In Search of Humanity,* 36–37.

6. See my article, "Experience and the Justification of Religious Belief," *Religious Studies* 17 (1981): 499–510.

10

The Defense of God: A Reprise
JOHN K. ROTH

Some realities are worth defending. Others are not. People put God in the latter category from time to time; however, most of this book's preceding discussion argues that, despite God's silence, men and women should rise to the defense of God. Yet the question remains: To what extent does God deserve defense? Opinion varies, and it should. For our experiences—especially those involving evil—are not the same. A Jewish survivor of Auschwitz, Elie Wiesel, knew as much when he reckoned that his people "will sooner or later be confronted with the enigma of God's action in history."[1] That enigma does not restrict itself to the Jews. In one way or another, as Wiesel also understands, it confronts us all.

Religion was not a sufficient condition for the Holocaust (the Nazi attempt to exterminate the Jews), but it was a necessary one. What happened at Auschwitz is inconceivable without beliefs about God held first by Jews and then by Christians. For many who live after Auschwitz, however, it is God not genocide that has been rendered inconceivable. At the very least, the Holocaust makes both Jewish and Christian religious affirmations more difficult and problematic than they were before. In an earlier day instances of natural destruction occupied much of the attention of philosophers and theologians. When considering, for example, the great earthquake that devastated Lisbon in the mid-eighteenth century, they argued whether such events could be reconciled with the claim that we live in the best of all possible worlds, or whether God could be regarded as both omnipotent and totally good. The Lisbon earthquake caused fires and floods. It killed thousands of people. It was also beyond human control. In centuries past, philosophers were well aware that catastrophes are also produced by human action, but their analyses often pivoted around natural disasters—"acts of God" as they were called—that human might could not prevent.

Nature's fury still demonstrates how fragile our lives can be. But today two factors stand out in bold relief. First, human beings do have considerable ability to control some of nature's destructive might. Death still claims everybody, but it need not come so quickly or painfully as in earlier times. If those results leave one to wonder why natural devastation has been so prevalent, they also testify that suffering can be reduced, that human life is not completely in the grip of necessities and inevitabilities which cannot be broken, and that affirmations about life's goodness can be underwritten by successes that make human existence more secure.

The second point, unfortunately, is less a cause for celebration. For if headway has been made against natural destruction that threatens human life, the problem of human self-destructiveness seems greater than ever. Ours is an age of redundant populations, refugees, concentration camps, and mass murder. It is capped by the ultimate dehumanizing threat: nuclear war. Violent deaths, caused by human catastrophes not by natural disasters, number well in the hundreds of millions in the twentieth century alone. The scale of man-made death, therefore, looms up as a fundamental fact to show conclusively that ours is not the best of all possible worlds.

The Holocaust is paradigmatic. It was not the result of sporadic, random violence carried out by hooligans. Driven by a zealous anti-Semitism, which seemed anything but irrational to the men who used it as a springboard to power, the Holocaust was a state-sponsored program of population elimination, a destruction process that could successfully target the Jews only because it received cooperation from every sector of German society. Why was this permitted to happen? That question indicts men and women, but since they did not begin history by themselves, the Holocaust makes that issue a religious one as well. What or who started history is a question without an answer, at least it is if by "answer" one means a human conclusion that is impregnable to doubt and completely certain. It is not, however, a question without answers; at least it is not if by "answers" one means convictions that people form, all of them fallible and possibly even false, to fathom their individual and collective experience. Weighing evidence differently, some of these beliefs are less affirmations in their own right and more rejections of claims held by others—as in atheism, for example—or manifestations of a refusal to affirm or reject—as in agnosticism—because too much knowledge is lacking. Over time many of a person's responses to religious questions and to questions about God in particular will change both in substance and in certitude.

Others will stay remarkably the same in spite of traumatic events that create great dissonance between what was believed before and what could possibly be accepted after.

The Holocaust qualifies as a watershed event. A typical reaction is to feel that Auschwitz seriously impugns the credibility of many, if not all, of the claims about God that Jews or Christians have usually made. Indeed, the Holocaust appears to call the very existence of God into a serious doubt, if it does not make God's nonexistence perfectly clear. Some would argue that it did not require the Holocaust to do these things. Previous human history contained far more than enough senseless injustice to demonstrate the delusions of trust in God. Such appraisals, however, do not give the Holocaust its due. Both in its own right and in the impact it bestows with its massive addition to history's accumulated waste, the Holocaust can shatter belief that had been able to endure more or less intact through everything else that went before. Theologians and philosophers who wish to defend Jewish or Christian views about God have always had a formidable task to show that God is not buried beneath history's debris. Few who enounter the Holocaust with seriousness would deny that any other reality makes their interpretive efforts more problematic than does Auschwitz.

As philosophers and theologians develop their points of view, they usually claim to ground their claims and arguments by appeals to actual human experience. Unavoidably these appeals go beyond direct knowledge of individual cases or the statistically documented studies of human behavior and belief carried out by social scientists. Philosophers and theologians draw on such materials, and on historical studies as well, but their efforts often require them to raise and reflect on questions that exceed immediate experience. The facts, it is often said, speak for themselves. They do not always speak clearly, however; nor are they self-interpreting. Philosophy and theology are disciplines that seek to interpret experience so that its most basic features—structural and normative—are clarified.

"Unique" and "unprecedented" are two of the descriptive terms most applied to the Holocaust. Jews in particular are likely to insist on using them, along with an emphasis on the particularistic nature of Nazi genocide, which specifically targeted Jews for total extermination root and branch simply because the Jews were Jews. Such emphases have validity and not least because they help to demonstrate that the Holocaust was a boundary-crossing event, one of those moments in history which changes everything before and after even if the substance and direction of the change takes time to dawn in consciousness. As philosophers and theologians probe the religious impact of the Holocaust, they can help to bring that dawning to fullness. They can also explore and indicate how it might be shaped, since the course of that dawning, like all human experience, remains subject to variation.

The first to probe the religious impact of the Holocaust, however, were not philosophers and theologians who thought about the Nazi onslaught after it had ceased. Men and women who lived and died and in some cases survived the hiding places, the ghettos, and the camps, already carried on that activity as their circumstances, energy, and inclination permitted. Their observations and feelings, expressed in diaries and eyewitness accounts, provide some of the most important experiential data for philosophers and theologians to encounter. For even if that data's religious testimony is not all that can or must be said on such matters, this testimony has an irreplaceable significance because it represents those who had to cope with genocide firsthand. To make pronouncements or even suggestions about what can or cannot, must or must not, be credible religiously after Auschwitz without knowing what the survivors think about their own experiences would be to develop one's philosophy or theology in a considerable vacuum.

Until recently, knowledge about the faith and doubt of Holocaust survivors had to rest largely on inferences drawn from oral and written testimony that remained scattered and unsystematically analyzed. There is still much work that should be done to gather this testimony, but thanks to the cooperation of many hundreds of survivors, a major social scientific study in this field is now available. During the 1970s, Reeve Robert Brenner polled a thousand Israeli survivors to ascertain the religious change, rejection, reaffirmation, doubt, and despair that the Holocaust might have brought them. Selecting the subjects at random from survivor rosters, especially from those carefully maintained at Yad Vashem, Israel's national Holocaust memorial, he received more than seven hundred responses to a lengthy questionnaire. Of those who responded, one hundred were interviewed personally, the remainder by mail. The data gathered is rich, the testimony moving. Much of it speaks about the silence of God, which is one way to designate what may be the most crucial religious problem posed by the Holocaust. How survivors have coped with that silence is instructive for the interpretive work that falls to philosophers and theologians today. No less so are some of Brenner's conclusions.

When Brenner speaks of "Holocaust survivors," he means Jews who successfully endured "various types of Nazi concentration camps, including detention or internment camps, transit and exchange camps, and annihilation or death camps where crematoria were installed."[2] Within his random and representative sample, one of the most fundamental findings is that 53 percent "consciously and specifically asserted that the Holocaust affected or, to a certain extent, modified their faith in God" (p. 103). The other 47 percent "averred that the Holocaust had no influence on their beliefs about God" (p. 95). Considering the cataclysmic qualities of the Holocaust, plus the fact that 69 percent of the surveyed survivors held that they had believed in God prior to the Holocaust, a figure that would have been another 10 percent higher for Eastern European Jews, the size of the 47 percent category may seem surprising. Brenner has no doubts that the survivors explored their religious histories profoundly and honestly in answering the wide-ranging and disturbing questions that he raised about religious behavior and belief before, during, and immediately after the Holocaust, and in the present as well. Nor does he regard the significant numbers of people—approximately one in four—who remained unwavering in their belief in the existence of God, personal or impersonal, as sufficient to modify his judgment that for those caught in the Holocaust "a radical transformation of faith took place" (p. 94). The most salient feature of this transformation is that of the 55 percent who before the Holocaust believed in "a personal God" who is involved in humanity's daily life, more than one in four rejected that belief either during or immediately after the war. Nor have they reclaimed it since (p. 94). At the heart of this rejection stands a fundamental premise, namely, that if there were a personal God who was involved in humanity's daily life, God would surely not cause or even permit an Auschwitz to exist.

Stubbornly powerful though it is, that assumption has not governed all theological reflection either during or after the Holocaust. In fact, Brenner's research found a vast array of religious responses among the survivors who responded. They included Orthodox Jews who say the Holocaust was God's punishment for Jewish refusal to honor the historic covenant with a God who made the Jews a chosen people. Others affirmed God but as One who is impersonal, uninvolved in human history generally or in the Holocaust specifically. And if nearly three out of four of the 53 percent who found their faith affected or modified by the Holocaust underwent "either a complete loss or an attenuation of religious faith," the remainder reported that the Holocaust made them more religious (pp. 103–4). Overall about 5 percent of all Brenner's sample were transformed from atheists into believers. If that figure seems insignificant, Brenner puts it in a different light by noting that "nearly one of every four religiously transformed survivors began to believe in God because of the Holocaust" (p. 119). That is, of those who moved from the basic position of affirming or denying the existence of God, the shifting was not exclusively, though largely, in one direction. Twenty-five percent of that group found themselves moved to affirm the existence of God when they had not done so before, and the impetus for that movement was the Holocaust itself. In all, Brenner observes, the total loss of faith in the existence of God among his sample of Holocaust survivors came to 11 percent.

Faith in God after Auschwitz is not easy for Holocaust survivors. For the questions that are felt about God's silence do not reach far until they ask: How can one believe in God at all after Auschwitz? Brenner found, however, that the believers' perplexity and discontent with their own beliefs had parallels in the experiences of those who professed atheism. Granted, those who sustained or arrived at atheism during the Holocaust were spared the frequently agonizing questions that Brenner's survey posed for those who affirmed God's reality. In some cases this atheism was strident, maintaining not merely that the existence of God, especially of the omnipotent God of Israel, is incredible but also that no theologian could possibly be qualified to controvert, let alone refute, that conclusion unless he or she had been through the "selection" itself. But Brenner found the atheism of others less self-assured. For some survivors, Brenner is convinced, profession of atheism was less a simple theological posture and more an emotional reaction, an expression of deep hurt and anger against God for leaving Jews so radically abandoned. Others found their atheism producing a sense of guilt. This was not guilt over having survived (Brenner's findings turned up very little of that syndrome), but rather a sense that one's atheism betrays too many of those who perished and even entails disloyalty to the Jewish tradition itself. At least for Jewish survivors, atheism after Auschwitz, however natural a response it may be, is rarely easy or comfortable.

If it is ironic that "those Holocaust survivors who became non-believers appear to feel the urgent need to explain and justify their non-belief to a far greater extent than believers seem to feel the need to justify *their* belief" (p. 112), still the believers are left to contend with demanding questions about the kind of God they affirm. Again, the variety of outlook is the most striking feature in Brenner's sample. Far from irresistably driving survivors away from belief in God, the Holocaust draws out many different views, thus suggesting that post-Holocaust religious options are not simply reducible to affirmation of one God or of none at all. It remains possible, of course, to label all affirmations of God incredible, and the Holocaust led significant numbers to do so. Along with the sheer diversity of affirmative views held by others, they underscore that no single idea about God will ever be acceptable to all. That same pluralism, however, means that the spectrum of what one may find religiously credible after Auschwitz remains open wide. One survivor's religious convictions do not necessarily speak for anyone else. Nor do those of philosophers or theologians who declaim for or against God in the Holocaust's aftermath. What such reflection can do is to help people confront the options so they can consider what honestly makes the most good sense. Survivors do this by showing how they personally have coped with massive destruction. Philosophers and theologians can share in that quest by developing various options in greater detail; by testing the alternatives critically as to their assumptions and implications; and by bringing imagination to bear to reinterpret religious traditions and to break new ground that reveals the significance of the Holocaust and the resources we need to reduce the waste that human power can churn out.

Survivors do not provide ultimate, final answers to complex questions raised by the Holocaust. No one can. The survivors' religious disagreement is substantial, but it is also worth noting that those who affirmed God's reality tended toward a consensus about views they *rejected*. None, for instance, regarded the Holocaust as evil that might really be good in disguise if viewed from a proper perspective. Nor did it seem to them that the Holocaust was a device used by God to refine or to purify moral character through suffering. Also unrepresented was the suggestion that there is an ultimate source of evil, a devil, who coexists with God: God may be the source of evil as well as of good, but God has no peers. At no time, moreover, did the survivors believe that Jews would finally disappear from the earth, and they welcomed the State of Israel as vindication of that trust. But likewise, when questioned whether Israel was worth the Holocaust, their collective response was, "If not a resounding and thunderous no, then certainly an emphatic no, a declination with little hesitation or uncertainty" (p. 246). Indeed if the State of Israel was insufficient to justify the Holocaust, not one "among these 708 twentieth-century Jewish victims . . . thought the world-to-come—whether as afterlife, heaven, messianic future, resurrection, or whatever a survivor may conceive—was sufficient alone to make sense out of the Holocaust" either (p. 206).

Although it does not follow that the survivors were equally unanimous in rejecting all affirmations of a world-to-come, they were nearly so in denying the theory that those who perished in the Holocaust were being punished by God for their own sinfulness. More than 70 percent of those who responded to that issue set aside any interpretation that linked the Holocaust to God's wrath or judgment in response to human sin. The Holocaust, they stressed, was humanity's doing, not God's. In emphasizing that point, however, the survivors recognized that the issue of God's relation to the Holocaust is not set aside. Their response to the following question, which merits quotation in full from Brenner's study, made that fact plain.

With regard to the destruction of the Six Million which one of these responses is the most acceptable to you?

a. It is inappropriate to blame God for the acts of man (man may decide to kill or not to kill).

b. It is not for us to judge the ways of God.

c. God was unable to prevent the destruction.

d. The Holocaust was the will of God (it was part of His divine plan).

e. Nothing can excuse God for not having saved them. (P. 215)

Of the 26 percent in Brenner's survey who chose not to answer this question, virtually all were nonbelievers. Among the remainder, the response most frequently chosen first (34 percent) was (b): it is inappropriate to judge God's ways. This option was followed closely (27 percent) by an emphasis on (a): refusal to blame God for what are human actions. One out of four put (e), the opposite of (a), in first place: God had no excuse for not saving the victims. Overall only 9 percent of the survivors stressed (d): the

Holocaust was God's will. Fewer still gave priority to (c): God was unable to prevent the Holocaust.

The configuration of first-choice emphases suggests that Holocaust survivors who believe in God take seriously the reality of human freedom and responsibility. Nonetheless, far from removing puzzles about God, that emphasis on freedom stands by another, namely, that it is not for us to judge the ways of God. But the latter response, implies ambivalence as much as piety. In spite of humanity's freedom, or even because of it, the ways of God remain puzzling in light of the Holocaust, an intimation that is reinforced by the fact that hardly any of the survivors would be prepared to place the primary emphasis theologically on the view that God was unable to prevent the destruction.

The opinions of Holocaust survivors are not necessarily normative theologically, but neither are they without significance when compared to some of the theological interpretations of the Holocaust that both Christians and Jews have offered recently. For in one way or another, those interpretations emphasize the very point that the survivors find immensely difficult to accept, namely, that God was somehow unable to prevent the destruction. On the Christian side, a noteworthy example is provided by Paul M. van Buren's *Discerning the Way: A Theology of the Jewish Christian Reality,* the first of a projected four-volume work. Engaged in a thoroughgoing re-evaluation of Christian thought in light of the Holocaust, the vigor of Jewish religious life throughout the centuries, and re-emergence of the State of Israel, van Buren does much to overcome Christian triumphalism and the notion that Christianity has superseded or negated Jewish faith. Unfortunately, his suggestions about God's relation to Auschwitz are far less credible than his estimates about how to reconceive the relations between Christians and Jews so that anti-Jewish sentiment in Christianity is laid to rest forever.

Van Buren's theology stresses that Christians worship the God of the Jews, the same God presumably who is the God of the survivors polled in Brenner's survey. Underscoring the difficulties of speaking about God at all after Auschwitz, van Buren tries to formulate a meaningful Christian response to the Holocaust. Like the survivors, van Buren stresses that God has created us free and responsible. To bestow us with those qualities, van Buren believes, is a loving thing for God to do. It also entails that God has "to sit still and to suffer in agony as His children move so slowly to exercise in a personal and loving way the freedom which He has willed for them to have and

exercise." Confronted by the question "Where was God at Auschwitz?", van Buren's understanding is that God was in the midst of
that destruction, suffering "in solidarity with His people." The
objectives of this suffering God, surmises van Buren, might have
included "trying to awaken His creatures to their irresponsibility.
Perhaps He was trying, by simply suffering with His people, to
awaken His church to a new understanding of love and respect for
them." Obviously uneasy about those answers, as well he might be,
van Buren adds: "The cost seems out of all proportion to the
possible gain, so silence may be the wiser choice" (p. 117). If so, van
Buren eschews it and goes on to elaborate his views about God's
suffering.

Those views amount to an apologetic defense of God predicated
on the assumption that God's creation of human freedom binds
God from decisive intervention in human affairs. God could not
intervene to stop the Holocaust, asserts van Buren, "without ceas-
ing to be the God of love and freedom who has . . . conferred
responsibility and free creative power on His creatures" (p. 119).
Here van Buren begs the question twice over. Responsibility and
free creative power are not incompatible with interventions by God
unless God or van Buren defines them that way. Moreover, if van
Buren or God does define them that way, then one might wonder
how that decision is supposed to embody love, seeing that its
outworkings in history led to unremitting slaughter in the Holocaust. Van Buren pleads that, if we are to think of God as a parental
figure (the imagery is common both in Judaism and Christianity),
"then this must surely be an agonizing period in God's life" (p. 153).
Well it might be, though less because of van Buren's emphasis that
God is bound by the existence of human freedom and more by
second thoughts about what God did in creating a world of freedom in which irresponsible destructiveness destroys more than love
appears to save.

About one matter van Buren is perfectly credible: "God is not a
God who does it all for His creatures" (p. 151). He may even be
correct that if more Christians had acknowledged that fact earlier,
millions murdered by Hitler might have been rescued. But if we are
to go on to suggest, as van Buren does, that the Holocaust becomes
divine revelation, informing us "that God requires that we take
unqualified responsibility before Him for His history with us" (p.
181), then at the very least common decency would seem to enjoin
us to ask God, or at least van Buren, whether there were not a more

effective, less wasteful way for God to get that message across. Van Buren reads the emergence of the State of Israel in a similar light. That development did occur because of human initiative, but to speak of such effort as containing revelation from God concerning human responsibility should raise still more questions about what God is doing. For however wonderful the State of Israel may be, the Holocaust survivors speak convincingly when they emphasize that in no way is it worth the price of the Holocaust, which has played such an unmistakable role in establishing and in sustaining the State of Israel.

Van Buren's Christian theology tries to retain a God whose goodness is as great as God's suffering and whose love is as vast as God's freedom. As far as history is concerned, however, his account gives God very little freedom. God's power recedes as humanity's emerges. A love that consists of suffering innocence remains. Van Buren believes that Christians take "the crucifixion to be God's greatest act," the very essence of suffering love (p. 115). But van Buren's perspective overlooks the fact that the crucifixion would have been just another Roman execution had it not been succeeded by what certain Jews took to be a substantial intervention in human affairs, namely, the resurrection of Jesus from death itself. At the very core of Christianity, and it poses a serious inconvenience for van Buren's Holocaust theology, is the assertion that God's divine power far exceeds anything that human beings can do. God is not bound by human freedom unless he wants to be. And if God wants to be, so that his presence at Auschwitz is that of suffering with the victims and not interceding on their behalf, then that is a problem for us all—God, Christians, Jews, and everybody else.

A credible Christian theology in a post-Holocaust world neither can nor will want to take God off the hook quite so easily as van Buren does, unless it is true that Christians are simply unwilling to confront the awesome and dreadful possibility that their God of love is at times needlessly and even wantonly involved with evil that did not have to be. "If we are to speak of ourselves as being responsible for history," writes van Buren, "then we shall have to find a way to speak of God that corresponds." (p. 99). True, people are responsible for history, but humanity's responsibility cannot be the whole story. It is irresponsible, not to say un-Christian, to assign responsibility inequitably. If God exists, God must bear a fair share. God's responsibility would be located in the fact that God is the one who ultimately sets the boundaries in which we live and move and have our being. Granted, since we are thrown into history at our birth, we appear in social settings made by human hands. But ultimately those hands cannot account for themselves. To the extent that they are born with the potential and the power to be dirty, credit for that fact belongs elsewhere. "Elsewhere" is God's address. Stendahl need not have been correct when he remarked that God's only excuse is that he does not exist. Still, to use human freedom and responsibility as a defense for God, we now ought to be mature enough to see, does not ring true. His establishment of that very freedom and responsibility, at least given the precise forms it has taken in history, rightly puts God on trial.

Van Buren remains exceedingly hopeful about human existence after the Holocaust. For having stressed God's limited intervening role in history, he still underscores that history shall be redeemed. To transform history into something very different from the slaughter-bench Hegel aptly envisioned it to be, some radical changes are going to be required. The issue is: Who will carry them out? By van Buren's reckoning, the burden of freedom places overwhelming responsibility on human shoulders, unless he reverses himself and suddenly falls back on a more dramatic divine intervention within history than his discerning of the ways of God provides a basis for expecting. For where is the evidence to suggest that, in a post-Holocaust world, human beings have made or are likely to make substantial progress in redeeming history? Who, in short, is going to do the redeeming? Van Buren puts little stock in secular humanity; its ways did too much to pave the way to Auschwitz. Christians, he notes, are declining in absolute numbers in the world. Perhaps, then, the task falls to the Jews. If it does, it is not likely that their human power alone will succeed in turning the world's swords into plowshares and its spears into pruning hooks. If lions and lambs are to lie down together in peace on this earth, nothing less than a massive intervention in history by God appears to be necessary. But given God's continued policy of non-intervention, the historical order will remain less than redeemed. God's promises for such renewal appear to be for "the life to come," if there is one. Meanwhile, Jews and Christians alike are left waiting to see what God's promises are made of, even as they themselves try to make the world less destructive.

The redemption of history is a theme with which post-Holocaust Jewish theologians must wrestle, too, for as Arthur A. Cohen argues in *The Tremendum: A Theological Interpretation of the Holo-*

caust, "redemption is Jewish."[4] That claim requires one to ask: What does redemption mean? Though Cohen underscores not only the Jewish roots of this idea but also that his understanding of redemption pertains to "the Jewish people, the House of Israel" (p. 108), his references to redemption are riddled with vagueness. Using the term much more than he defines it, Cohen implies that redemption entails more than continuing Jewish existence. That element—he sometimes refers to the "eternal" existence of the Jews—is absolutely fundamental, but Cohen goes on to employ the term in additional ways. For example, "there is," he says, "no portion of the human earth that does not need redemption in order that growth be renewed" (p. 109). He also speaks of "the promise of redemption" and later of "the last minute of redemption" (pp. 84, 110). He comes closest to clarifying the meaning of such language when he alludes to "the binding up and healing, not of persons, but of peoples," but little elaboration follows concerning how those ideas should be construed (p. 108). Apparently this binding up and healing are to be actions within history, but the extent to which they can achieve fulfillment there remains obscure. That outcome is not owing entirely to Cohen's verbal imprecision. It depends more decisively on the Holocaust itself.

Cohen has his own name for the Holocaust. He calls it the *tremendum.* This word, he hopes, will signify a sense of immensity, "a horror that exceeds the category of horror" (p. 31), an event within history but whose "reality exceeds its causalities (p. 6). The Holocaust, Cohen asserts, "ended forever one argument of history—whether the Jews are a chosen people. They are chosen, unmistakably, extremely, utterly" (p. 11). As Jews were brought to the borders of extinction, a moral and religious abyss ultimately scarred existence. The abyss engulfs redemption. For if the Holocaust and its aftermath reveal advances in technical competence, they unmask the pretension in assertions that "the world grows better or that mankind improves" (p. 47). Yet, insists Cohen, the ultimacy of the Holocaust is not to be confused with finality. Ultimate in its "consummate destructiveness" (p. 48), the Holocaust is not necessarily final (the latter term referring to whether consummate destructiveness is the destiny of human existence and of Jewish life in particular). The ultimacy of the Holocaust, thinks Cohen, is sufficient to require "a redefinition of the reality of God and his relations to the world and man" (p. 84). That redefinition, he recognizes more profoundly than van Buren, must reckon with the fact that God "creates a universe in which such destructiveness occurs" (p. 82). But then Cohen, too, evades the implication that is apparently too scandalous to escape silence, namely, that God is needlessly involved in destruction that is indeed ultimate if not final.

Instead Cohen offers a romanticized God, plus some recommendations for calming spirits troubled by their encounters with divinity during and after Auschwitz. "Creation," holds Cohen, "is necessity within God," whose "being is full and plenteous" (p. 90). God is a never-diminished source of "new forms, new beginnings" (p. 91). Human rationality and freedom are God's creation, but if God is the source of all historical possibilities, men and women are the ones who enact them. And this enactment is really ours, which is to say that no divine intervention is to be expected. To wish otherwise seriously, Cohen contends, would be to assume "that the created world is never independent of God" or to deny human life "its essential freedom" (p. 96). But surely this false dichotomy does not exhaust the possibilities, especially if we are dealing with a God whose range of possibilities, no less than God's being itself, is full and plenteous. In what sense is a freedom that creates Cohen's *tremendum* to be construed as "essential?" To hold that it is simply begs the question. As for "independent," that term's meanings are neither single nor fixed—least of all, one would assume, for God. To rule out God's intervention in history is to stipulate a meaning for independence and a status for the world that may or may not be the case.

Even more intriguing, as Cohen pens his paean to God's on-going and ever-new creative action, the connections between those aspects and the hideously bloody history that results recede from view. Granted, Cohen says that "the *tremendum* remains *tremendum*, neither diminished nor explained," but then he urges his readers to see that God's "plentitude and unfolding are the hope of our futurity." If we can do so, he urges, "we shall have won a sense of God whom we may love and honor, but whom we no longer fear and from whom we no longer demand" (pp. 95–97). The problem that remains, however, is what the plentitude and unfolding of God still have in store. Underscoring that "the historical is the domain of human freedom" (p. 98), what is in store within history will fall largely to human determination. Here Cohen falls prey to the same probability that ruins van Buren's hopes for redemption within history, namely, that there is precious little evidence to convince perceptive judgment that humanity's wasting of life will decline, not to say disappear. That situation, in turn, ultimately traces back to God as the source of our possibilities. The ways in which Cohen's God is involved in history do not make clear that God deserves only love and honor. Nor does it follow, if we are to speak in those terms, that we love and honor such a God well if all elements of fear and of holding God to account are removed. Thanks to God, as well as to ourselves, the chances here and now of binding up and really healing the wounds inflicted by history appear to be slim—short of a massive intervention on God's part, which seems not to be in the cards either.

Cohen argues that the Holocaust is not final. Yes, life—including Jewish life—does go on, but the issue is whether anything can happen in this world or in the world to come that will lead us to set aside a judgment that may well be final because it is ultimately true: Human life has emerged within boundaries set by God that make needless waste and wanton destruction all too real. Perhaps in "the last minute of redemption," to use Cohen's phrase, God will erase every memory of the Holocaust and win the ovation of love and honor that Cohen wants for him. Short of such action, the ultimacy of the Holocaust remains to impinge on finality. One element of that finality is that God's world needlessly contained a Holocaust that God, if not humanity, could have avoided.

If so, honor and love for God are not necessarily eliminated, though they are rendered difficult, and the difficulties can be sufficient to move people away from belief in a personal God or in any God at all, as the testimony of survivors indicates. In my view, then, credible post-Holocaust honor and love for God, if they occur at all, will need to include being for God by being against God, too. This response confesses that God's power is decisive if destruction and death are not to be final. But the same affirmation recognizes that power sufficient to deny finality to destruction and death can be bound by no necessity that makes it powerless to stop a Holocaust.

Arthur Cohen is correct: The Holocaust makes "the sovereignty of evil" seem "more real and immediate and familiar than God" (p. 34). He is correct again when he asserts: "The question . . . is not how can God abide evil in the world, but how can God be affirmed meaningfully in a world where evil enjoys such dominion" (p. 34). Neither van Buren's suffering God nor Cohen's God of plenteous unfolding fully meets that test. To protect their fundamental goodness, the Gods of these theologians are hamstrung necessarily by human freedom; and yet, even though it cannot be utilized now, they retain power sufficient to assure that redemption will finally arrive. No Holocaust survivor is likely to be swayed by such theological subtleties. They are essentially apologetic attempts to calm dissonance that is never likely to go away after Auschwitz because the feelings in which it roots are deeper-seated, more stubborn, and perhaps more honest than any of our theological theories.

That dissonance can be summed up in a few words: If a caring God exists, why didn't that God stop the Holocaust when human beings failed so miserably to do so? To say that God could not stop it is an answer that arouses suspicion at least as much as it lays gut-level questions to rest. For those who cannot lay those questions and suspicions to rest, one alternative will be to deny God or at least to deny that God cares. Another moves in a different direction. It admits that our highest hopes are dashed: Things are not going to work out for the best. Still, they might work out better instead of worse, and since we know that life can be very good—else why the dismay and anger when things turn out otherwise?—then the Holocaust can lead us to stand against despair by affirming that God can stop evil whenever and wherever God chooses to do so. But in doing so men and women also choose the hardest path: For the choice is not only for God when there may be none, or at least none that cares, but also for a God whose goodness is less than perfect because God's involvement with evil is at times more than we can bear. To hope in this God is also to protest against God and vice versa. The significance of this position, it should be emphasized, is *not* to blame God as a way of covering up our human responsibilities, but rather to intensify honesty with God and with ourselves as a means to deepen compassion for the world. Such positions are taken at the risk of being defeated, but they may also be vindicated. In either case they at least have the decency not to defend God at humanity's expense, and not to place God's portion of responsibility on human shoulders when the portion that is rightfully ours, limited though it is, is still more than we typically handle as well as we might.

By Reeve Robert Brenner's reckoning, it should be remembered, "nearly three of every four survivors were of the conviction that the Six Million were destroyed only as a consequence of man's inhumanity to man and with no connection whatever to God."[5] Clearly, in one way or another the Holocaust has diminished our sense of God's presence in history. Yet the fact remains that human existence does not account for itself. That fact is enough to keep at least the question of God in our midst. Insofar as the question of God remains alive in the survivor community polled by Brenner, it bears remembering that only 5 percent "were of the conviction that 'God could not have prevented the Holocaust.' . . . For most other survivors, 'a God who is not all-powerful is not God at all'" (p. 231). The views of these survivors are neither normative nor binding on anyone. They may even need to be rejected. At the very least, however, they convincingly drive home that religious questions about the Holocaust have everything to do with power. As we continue to wrestle with the silence of God, the survivors' testimony is a reminder that the power equation between God and humanity should remain at issue in a world where the Holocaust has happened. Van Buren and Cohen contribute to that understanding, too. By focusing reasons for agreement or disagreement with them, each of us can better discern our way in interpreting what the Holocaust can and cannot, must and must not, mean. In doing so, we should learn not to say too much—or too little—in the defense of God.[6]

NOTES

1. Elie Wiesel, *One Generation After,* trans. Lily Edelman and the author (New York: Avon Books, 1972), 215.

2. Reeve Robert Brenner, *The Faith and Doubt of Holocaust Survivors,* (New York: The Free Press, 1980), 21.

3. Paul M. van Buren, *Discerning the Way: A Theology of the Jewish Christian Reality* (New York: Seabury Press, 1980), 116.

4. Arthur A. Cohen, *The Tremendum: A Theological Interpretation of the Holocaust* (New York: Crossroad, 1981), 108.

5. Brenner, 230.

6. An earlier edition of this essay appeared in *Faith and Philosophy* 1 (1984): 407–20.

Notes on the Contributors

BOWMAN L. CLARKE is professor of philosophy at the University of Georgia, Athens, Georgia. He is author of *Language and Natural Theology* and co-editor of *God and Temporality*. He is also editor of the *International Journal for Philosophy of Religion*.

LLOYD EBY is lecturer in philosophy at the Unification Theological Seminary, Barrytown, New York. Now completing his Ph.D. at Fordham University, Bronx, New York, his dissertation is entitled *Objective Knowledge and the Knowing Subject: The Popper-Kuhn Debate*.

FRANK R. HARRISON, III, is professor of philosophy at the University of Georgia, Athens, Georgia. His primary area of interest is twentieth-century English philosophy. He is author of *Deductive Logic and Descriptive Language*.

ADRIO KÖNIG is head of the Department of Systematic Theology and Theological Ethics at the University of South Africa, Pretoria, South Africa. In addition to his extensive publications in Afrikaans, two of his major works have been translated into English: *Here Am I* and *Introduction to Theology*.

EUGENE T. LONG is professor of philosophy at the University of South Carolina, Columbia, South Carolina. Concentrating on phenomenology, existentialism, and the philosophy of religion, he is the author of *Jaspers and Bultmann: A Dialogue between Philosophy and Theology in the Existentialist Tradition*.

MARTIN PROZESKY is associate professor of religious studies at the University of Natal, Pietermaritzburg, South Africa. His first book, *Religion and Ultimate Well-Being: An Explanatory Theory* was published in 1984.

KLAUS A. ROHMANN, a specialist on contemporary religious thought, is professor of theology at the Catholic College of Social Sciences in Osnabrück and Vechta, West Germany. Among his publications is *Vollendung im Nichts?: Eine Dokumentation der Amerikanischen Gott-ist-Tot-Theologie.*

JOHN K. ROTH is the Russell K. Pitzer Professor of Philosophy at Claremont McKenna College, Claremont, California. He recently served as visiting professor of Holocaust Studies at the University of Haifa, Israel. His ten books include *A Consuming Fire: Encounters with Elie Wiesel and the Holocaust.*

JÖRG SALAQUARDA is on the faculty of religious studies at Johannes Gutenberg University, Mainz, Bad Nauheim, West Germany. Exploring the history of philosophy and religious thought, his publications include *Philosophische Theologie in Schatten des Nihilismus* and the German translation of Walter Kaufmann's *Nietzsche: Philosopher, Psychologist, Antichrist* (4th ed.).

FREDERICK SONTAG is the Robert C. Denison Professor of Philosophy at Pomona College, Claremont, California. The author of nearly twenty books on philosophy and religious thought, his most recent is *The Elements of Philosophy.*

INDEX

Abraham, earth blessed through, 28
Acquinas, Saint Thomas, 9–10, 38–39
Acts of the Apostles, 120
Adam, 54–57
Advaita Hinduism, 106
Adventures of Ideas (Whitehead), 43–44
Altman, Robert, 50
Amos, 23, 68
Anselm, Saint, 1, 121
anthropocentrism, 128, 129–130
anthropogenesis, 97, 99
anthropology, Marxian, 92, 93
apologia, 120–121, 123
Aristotle, 9
atheism, 87–88, 89, 127, 153–154
Augustine, Saint, 9–10, 128
authentic relations, 142–143

Babel, today's world likened to,
  68–69
Babylonia:
  deities of, 15, 17, 24
  exile of Israel in, 21, 22–24
Bacon, Francis, 129
basic bits of knowledge, 71–72
Benedictines, work as viewed by,
  128–129
Bergman, Ingmar, 50
blacks, religious vitality of, 9
Bloch, Ernst, 94–95
Book of Common Prayer, 114
Brenner, Reeve Robert, 151–156, 163,
  164
Bresson, Robert, 50
Brothers Karamazov, The
  (Dostoevsky), 44–45, 48
Buddhism:

and common suffering of all creatures, 94
immanence and transcendence in,
  145
Buñuel, Luis, 50

Calvin, John, 9–10
Cambodia, communist tyranny in, 51
Camus, Albert, 48, 61, 62, 64
Canaanite deities, 15
Capra, Frank, 50
catechism, argument of repression
  and, 88
certainty, 80
  perspective thinking and, 122–123
Chalcedonian Christology, 111, 112
China, communist tyranny in, 51
Christianity:
  apologia in, 120–121, 123
  and dominion over the earth,
    127–130
  and grace of God, 139
  Holocaust and, 156–159
  kingdom of God in, 94
Clarke, Bowman L., viii, 32–47
clerical deception, hypothesis of,
  88–90, 93
Cocteau, Jean, 50
cognitional analysis, 111
Colossians, 31
committed view of life, 140–141
Communist Manifesto (Marx and
  Engels), 13
conversions, religious, 137
Coppola, Francis Ford, 50
1 Corinthians, 31, 121
Creation story, 8–9, 25, 29–30
  Unification account of, 54–55

Index

Index

Index

Index

and development of science,
126–127
dominium terrae and, 127–130
emergence of, 121–123
religious thinking and, 123–127
teleology and, 131–133
Peter, Saint, 2, 120
1 Peter, 120
Petrarch, 121
Pharaoh, plagues against, 22
Pharisees, Jesus vs., 29
phenomonology of existence of
being, 139
Pike, Nelson, 38, 39
Pilate, Pontius, 126
Plato, 9, 49, 85
Pocket Theology (Holbach), 88
Portrait of the Artist as a Young Man, A
(Joyce), 50
Potok, Chaim, 50
probability, knowledge and, 70–71
Providence of Restoration, 59
Prozesky, Martin, ix-x, 102–119
Psalms, 17, 30, 124
purposeful action, 72

Qur'an, 102, 112

reality:
alternative approach to, 74–81
God and, 72–73, 82–83
idol of, 70–74
Red Sea, delivery at, 22
Reimarus, Hermann Samuel, 125
relation consciente, 122, 124
religion(s):
as accident of birth, 137
actions taken in name of, 4–5, 7,
10–12, 13–14
and argument of repression, 84–101
and arts, 50
and committed view of life, 140–141
common ground among, 142
criteriology of, 106–110
Darwinism vs., 51
defense of God central to, 6–7, 11,
13–14
Enlightenment and, 5, 88
and expectations of future, 8, 9

faith vs. belief in, 141–142
Freud vs., 51–52
happiness vs., 49–50
indictments against, 49–52, 64–65
infighting among, 4, 7, 13–14, 52,
135
judging of, 102–119
manifesto of, 13–14
Marxism vs., 51, 91–95
as mediator between God and man,
53
philosophy vs., 52
reasons for resort to, 5
syncretism of, 136
transformation of, 116–119
uncertainty and, 123–126
Renaissance, perspective thinking in,
121–122
repentance, exclusivity of God and, 15
repression, argument of, 84–101
clerical deception as basis of, 88–90,
93
historical materialism and, 90–95
self-control and, 95–100
Rocky II, 50
Rohmann, Klaus A., x, 120–134
Romans, 29, 30, 133
Rosen, Nathan, 62
Roth, John K., x-xi, 148–164
Rowley, H. H., 21–22
Russell, Bertrand, 41–42

Salaquarda, Jörg, ix, 84–101
1 Samuel, 28
Satan, 56, 57, 59
Saviors of God, The (Kazantzakis), 6
Science and the Modern World
(Whitehead), 41, 43
selfhood, 132
self-reflexivity, 78, 79, 81
sensory perception, 80
sexual relations, Unification theology
and, 55, 56, 59
Sinai, revelation at, 21
*Sister Mary Ignatius Explains It All For
You* (Durang), 49–50
Sisyphus, 86
Smart, Ninian, 139
Smith, Ronald Gregor, 138
Smith, Wilfred Cantwell, 141–142
Socrates, 33, 49, 85

Index